NO LAND!
NO HOUSE!
NO VOTE!

Voices from
Symphony Way

Through the voices of the peoples of Africa and the global South, Pambazuka Press and Pambazuka News disseminate analysis and debate on the struggle for freedom and justice.

Pambazuka Press – www.pambazukapress.org

 A Pan-African publisher of progressive books and DVDs on Africa and the global South that aim to stimulate discussion, analysis and engagement. Our publications address issues of human rights, social justice, advocacy, the politics of aid, development and international finance, women's rights, emerging powers and activism. They are primarily written by well-known African academics and activists. All books are available as ebooks.

Pambazuka News – www.pambazuka.org

 The award-winning and influential electronic weekly newsletter providing a platform for progressive Pan-African perspectives on politics, development and global affairs. With more than 2,500 contributors across the continent and a readership of more than 660,000, Pambazuka News has become the indispensable source of authentic voices of Africa's social analysts and activists.

Pambazuka Press and Pambazuka News are published by Fahamu (www.fahamu.org)

NO LAND!
NO HOUSE!
NO VOTE!

Voices from Symphony Way

Written and edited
by the Symphony Way
Pavement Dwellers

Pambazuka Press

Published 2011 by Pambazuka Press, an imprint of Fahamu
Cape Town, Dakar, Nairobi and Oxford
www.pambazukapress.org www.fahamubooks.org www.pambazuka.org

Fahamu, 2nd floor, 51 Cornmarket Street, Oxford OX1 3HA, UK
Fahamu Kenya, PO Box 47158, 00100 GPO, Nairobi, Kenya
Fahamu Senegal, 9 Cité Sonatel 2, POB 25021, Dakar-Fann, Dakar, Senegal
Fahamu South Africa, c/o 19 Nerina Crescent, Fish Hoek, 7975 Cape Town, South Africa

First published 2011

British Library Cataloguing in Publication Data
A catalogue record for this book is available from the British Library

ISBN: 978-1-906387-84-6 paperback
ISBN: 978-0-85749-030-8 ebook – pdf

Printed by National Printing Press, Bangalore, India

Contents

When they evicted us,
I just lost it. Those same
policemen couldn't arrest my
child's murderer, but they can
kick us poor people out of the
only houses we have...

Symphony Way resident

Acknowledgements

Translators and Afrikaans supporting editors

Bonita Jubelin
Christabel Small
John Schultz
Evelyn McQuena

Primary editors

Each resident edited their own story

Supporting editor

Jared Sacks

Photographers

The Symphony Way children with a few special photos from Lolos Engelbrecht (6 years old)
Zainodien Linneveldt from Symphony Way
Outside photographers: Roe Yardini, Laura Huss, Jared Sacks, Kerry Chance, Valentina Iacoponi
A particular thanks to all the photographers from Symphony Way whom we are unable to name

Special thanks

A special thanks to Matt Birkinshaw, Raj Patel, Jared Sacks and the dedicated activists of the Symphony Way Anti-Eviction Campaign who made this book possible and helped bring the struggle forward

Pambazuka Press wishes to acknowledge the support of the following for the publication of this book:

Glossary of people, places and terms

AEC or WC-AEC   The Western Cape Anti-Eviction Campaign is a community-based and community-controlled movement bringing together over 15 community organisations, crisis committees and concerned residents' groups to realise our right to land, housing, basic services and democratic decision-making. We are not affiliated with any politician, political party or NGO. We declare No Land! No House! No Vote! We speak only for ourselves but we struggle for liberation and change for everyone everywhere.

aluta continua   From the Portuguese phrase *a luta continua*, meaning 'the struggle continues', a term that became a popular rallying cry during the independence struggle in Mozambique. It was appropriated by anti-apartheid activists and is now used by poor South Africans struggling against the current government.

amandla ngawethu   A phrase in isiXhosa and isiZulu that means 'power to us'. It was a popular rallying cry during resistance against apartheid and is still used today among South African social movements such as the Anti-Eviction Campaign.

Ameen   An Islamic religious term that is the same as the Christian term 'Amen', which means 'We agree'.

badtjie   Washing basin.

Blikkiesdorp or Blikkies   A 'blik' is the Afrikaans word for a 'tin'. 'Blikkiesdorp', which translates as 'Tin-can Town', is the nickname given by the Symphony Way community to the Symphony Way Temporary Relocation Area (TRA). It is the name now used by Blikkiesdorp residents themselves, the media and even some government officials. This TRA is built and managed by the Democratic Alliance-led City of Cape Town as a place to put internal refugees from the violent N2 Gateway evictions of February 2008. Blikkiesdorp is criticised for its high crime rate, barbed-wire fencing, police-controlled access to the camp and its erosion of social networks. The City of Cape Town has attempted to forcibly remove the residents of Symphony Way and put them in Blikkiesdorp.

Boere   The official definition of 'Boere' or 'Boer' or 'Afrikaner' is a South African of Dutch extraction. However, South Africa's poor non-white populations use the term to refer to the current South African police. Residents call them the 'boere' because the 'integrated' police force currently carries out similar acts of oppression to those of the Afrikaner government during apartheid.

Caspar The notorious armed vehicles used by apartheid-era police and security forces to break up anti-apartheid protests and riots. Still used in post-apartheid South Africa, there were four Caspars present during the N2 Gateway evictions.

Deen A Muslim word for religion or faith.

dom A widely used South African slang term originating from Afrikaans which translates as 'dumb' or 'stupid'.

Richard Dyantyi A former member of the Executive Council (MEC) for local government and housing in the Western Cape Province. He oversaw the N2 Gateway project and the violent evictions in February 2008. He was fired from his position on 31 July 2008.

galies Small metal bins used to make fires on Symphony Way.

gatvol Fed up.

hoender netjies Afrikaans for 'chicken necks'.

hokkie or **hok** An Afrikaans word that directly translates into English as 'box' but is used as slang for a 'shack'.

Insha-Allahan An Islamic term that literally means 'God willing' or 'may God grant you that wish'.

Whitey Jacobs A former member of the Executive Council (MEC) for housing in the Western Cape Province. He took over after 31 July 2008 and was removed when the Democratic Alliance won control of the province on 8 May 2009. While he held a number of meetings with anti-eviction communities, Symphony Way families accuse him of breaking numerous promises to provide housing for residents.

kimbies Disposable nappies.

kwaai Dangerous, although also used as slang for 'cool'.

kwela-kwela 'Kwela' is township slang derived from Zulu and means 'get up'. Kwela-kwela is a slang term for the Caspar armed vehicles used during apartheid and today.

Law Enforcement (see also Police and Metro Police) Law Enforcement's mandate is limited to enforcing city-enacted by-laws. A subdivision of Law Enforcement is the city's notorious Anti-Land Invasions Unit. These officials are often accused of working beyond their mandate.

lekker 'Tasteful/tastefully' and 'nice/nicely' when referring to food, but often used to refer to other things.

Frank Martin The Democratic Alliance (DA) councillor for the 19th ward in Cape Town (which includes Blue Downs, Kuilsriver, Wesbank and a small eastern section of Delft). Martin was accused of using his position to stoke racial anger amongst 'Coloured' backyard residents of Delft and, with the

DA's tacit support, gave families permission to occupy over 1,500 N2 Gateway houses (see the letter to Auntie Cynthie, page 66). Afterwards, Martin refused to support the families in public, claiming that he never gave them permission to occupy the homes.

Dan Plato   Mayor of the City of Cape Town.

Metro Police (see also Police and Law Enforcement)   Metro Police are different from the South African Police Service (SAPS) in that they are a local police service under the control of the local municipality. They focus primarily on traffic services and enforcing general laws. They have some powers similar to the SAPS but their powers are limited.

mos   A slang filler word, inviting agreement from the listener, e.g. 'You understand, mos' means 'You understand, don't you?'.

No Land! No House! No Vote!   The name of a national pro-democracy campaign renouncing party politics, boycotting the vote and challenging vote banking in South Africa. The name implies that because government does not deliver on issues important to affected communities (such as land and housing) these communities will not vote. But the slogan goes farther than this in demanding the right and responsibility for communities to be involved in setting policies and issues themselves rather than having to rely on politicians and personalities to make decisions for them.

nother   Nothing.

Opel   The name of a General Motors subsidary company that makes many of the cars sold in South Africa.

pangas   Machetes.

Police (see also Law Enforcement and Metro Police)   In South Africa, 'police' generally refers to the South African Police Service (SAPS).

POW camp   A prisoner-of-war camp is a site for the containment of combatants captured by their enemy in time of war. It is similar to an internment camp which is used for civilian populations.

sail   A plastic covering often used to cover roofs and prevent water and wind from coming through.

SAP/SAPS   After 1994, the government changed the name of the South African Police to the South African Police Service in order to distinguish the latter from the former, which was notorious for its apartheid-era atrocities. In this book, residents use both abbreviations interchangeably because they see little difference between the two in terms of how the service treats them.

Tokyo Sexwale   Minister of human settlements in the national government.

skwatter   Slang for squatter.

stragel Struggle.

structure The term commonly used amongst residents to refer to a shack, hokkie, blikkie or any type of substandard housing.

stuk kak Piece of shit.

swote Shot.

taaiers Afrikaans for 'tyres'.

Temporary Relocation Area (TRA) Also known as a Transit Camp or Decant Camp in other parts of South Africa, this is a government-built holding area for poor South Africans who have been moved from another location. TRAs are generally used to house South Africa's unwanted urban poor in boondocks areas away from profitable development sites.

Thubelisha Thubelisha Homes is the name of the section 21 not-for-profit company appointed to manage the N2 Gateway Housing Project. The name has now become synonymous with privatisation-related corruption in the housing sector. Thubelisha was declared insolvent in 2009 and was replaced by/transformed into the National Housing Agency.

Tsunami The name of a TRA in Delft which is used primarily to house victims of the 2005 fire in the Joe Slovo Informal Settlements. Residents of Tsunami have not been allowed to return to Joe Slovo, where government housing has been built. Current Joe Slovo residents are resisting attempts by the government to forcibly remove them to Delft TRAs such as Tsunami.

ubuntu An African philosophy which speaks about a common humanity where a person gains their life-worth through their interactions with other people.

VAT Value Added Tax, a kind of sales tax which is regressive and most burdensome for the poor.

vrek Too expensive.

voetsek Literally 'put your foot in a sack', it means 'go away' when translated and is used interchangeably with 'fuck off'. The word is very degrading and used primarily when speaking to dogs or other animals.

WC-AEC Western Cape Anti-Eviction Campaign (see AEC above).

Helen Zille Former mayor of the City of Cape Town and the current premier of the Western Cape.

Foreword

Raj Patel

Every day, watching your dream-house from behind the apartheid fence

FOR THOSE OUTSIDE South Africa, particularly for the generation of activists who fought apartheid, it's tempting to imagine that after Mandela was freed from Robben Island and lines snaked outside polling booths in the first free elections, after the ANC won and the national anthem became 'Nkosi Sikelele Afrika', and after Nelson Mandela held high the Rugby World Cup trophy, that even while the Soviet Union collapsed and capitalism crowed triumphantly from the United States, all was well in the Rainbow Nation.

But despite the close-harmony singing and the holding aloft of leaders, South Africa isn't *The Lion King*. It's more like *Animal Farm*. Orwell ends *Animal Farm* with a scene in which we see the pigs and the humans whom they had displaced sharing a meal together. At this point in the text, it becomes difficult to tell pig from human. Over the past two decades, a few black South Africans have become very wealthy, as Steve Biko had predicted in 1972:

> This is one country where it would be possible to create a capitalist black society, if whites were intelligent, if the nationalists were intelligent. And that capitalist black society, black middle class, would be very effective … South Africa could succeed in putting across to the world a pretty convincing, integrated picture, with still 70 per cent of the population being underdogs.

For many, the struggle against apartheid never ended, because the ethos of apartheid continues to live. Poor blacks still live in segregated sprawling townships far from the wealthy (still mostly white) suburbs. The introduction of neoliberal economic policies in the 1990s has led to falling levels of social welfare and an increase in the cost of living for the poorest. In South Africa, human development levels are now lower than in Palestine. Poor South Africans live shorter life-spans and are more financially insecure than before 1994.[1]

The ascent of a new black capitalist class isn't, however, the end of the narrative. The state itself, in trying to stamp out the uncomfortable appearance of poverty and in behaving in ways similar to the apartheid regime, has done much to fan the flames of dissent and to continue the story of the fight against apartheid. Indeed, there is an average of about 15 protests held in South Africa every day, with about 20 per cent being banned by the current government.[2]

Think, for instance, of the hundreds of families living in backyards across the new township of Delft in Cape Town, who thought that Christmas had come early in 2007. They received letters from their local councillor inviting them to move into houses they had been waiting for since the end of apartheid. They left their backyard shacks, to occupy their new homes in the flagship national N2 Gateway Housing Project. Then, on Christmas Eve, the police moved in with their Caspars, their riot gear and their rubber bullets. Despite the violence, the families were able to stay in their homes because of a last-minute high court interdict preventing the government from evicting the families without a court order.

For a brief moment, all was as well as could be expected. Since the homes lacked doors and windows, families outfitted their houses themselves. Some families even began planting their own vegetable gardens. The quality of housing in the N2 project is an ongoing scandal, but at least the homes were theirs.

Then the families received another notice. They were to be evicted and thrown onto the streets despite the right to housing being enshrined in South Africa's constitution. The original letters authorising them to move into their new homes had been sent illegally. The local councillor who sent them suffered the modest indignity of being suspended for a month. But he kept his job and is now being silently promoted within his political party.

The N2 residents were treated altogether more harshly. In February 2008, they were kicked out of their homes with nowhere to go – their former backyard shacks having been rented to new families the moment the old ones left. At least 20 residents, women and children, were shot with rubber bullets while peacefully protesting the eviction. A three-year-old child was shot three times and almost lost his life.

The families' new homes became the sandy embankments next to the road directly opposite the housing project. Hundreds of these residents organised themselves into the Symphony Way Anti-Eviction Campaign, built shacks for

their families and vowed to stay on the road until the government gave them permanent housing. The city temporarily blocked off Symphony Way to traffic. Yet when cars and minibuses pushed through the barriers, the pavement dwellers enacted their own permanent road blockade. Lasting almost two years, this act of civil disobedience became one of the longest-running protest campaigns in the country's history.

By the beginning of 2009, the City of Cape Town was trying to force them into a temporary relocation area (TRA) it had built to hold the victims of the February 2008 evictions. The units that pass for housing here are tin shacks, 'blikkies', ramshackle blocks of zinc sheets in the sand. The transit camp is plagued by gale-force winds and baking sun, sealed in by armed police yet beset with crime. Commentators have described the TRA as a concentration camp; a place to put poor, marginalised South Africans.[3] The City of Cape Town is now using the TRA as a dumping site for the homeless and street children. They are seen as an eyesore in the city centre, particularly during the 2010 football World Cup.[4]

But the Symphony Way families refused to move to 'Blikkiesdorp'. They continued to organise – holding protests, setting up a makeshift office, opening their own crèche. The city refused to negotiate with residents over other options, such as the numerous unoccupied pieces of land nearby. They claimed that the only possible alternative accommodation was this 'camp'.

Then the government threw its might into the legal system, extracting an eviction order that required all 136 families to move to the sandy wastes of Blikkiesdorp by October 2009, just in time for the tin shacks to bake in the summer heat.

Blikkiesdorp (frontside). The camp, with 24-hour police-controlled entry

Apartheid ends and apartheid remains[5]

The squires of the new order bicker among themselves for the spoils.

The poor, who fought and died for justice, wait for it long after its arrival has been announced. Movements arise to hasten the day when apartheid's remains can be swept away. The movements are, so it seems, crushed. At the beginning of 2010, when this foreword was being written, the South African government had gone on the offensive against organisations of poor people across the country, from refugee camps of foreign nationals,[6] to ANC-affiliated mob attacks against the leadership of the Kennedy Road Development Committee in Durban,[7] to the residents of Symphony Way in Cape Town.

So why should you care about the pavements of Symphony Way when there's no one there anymore (just in time to open the road for the 2010 World Cup)? The readiest answer is that while the government can take the people out of Symphony Way, they can't take Symphony Way out of the people. As the residents themselves announced,

> Symphony Way is not dead. We are still Symphony Way. We will always be Symphony Way. We may not be living on the road, but our fight for houses has only just begun. We warn government that we have not forgotten that they have promised us houses and we, the Symphony Way Anti-Eviction Campaign, will make sure we get what is rightfully ours.[8]

This book is testament to what it is to be Symphony Way. Written toward the end of the struggle on the pavements, this anthology of letters is both testimony and poetry. The power of the words comes not simply from confession, but through the art with which these stories are told.

Every struggle has its narrators, but some on Symphony Way are wordsmiths of the highest order. When Conway Payn (page 119) invites you to 'put your shoes into my shoes and wear me like a human being would wear another human being', he opens the door to a world of compassion and fellow-suffering that holds you firm.

The letters do not make for easy reading. Lola Wentzel's story of the Bush of Evil (page 15), of the permanent geography of sexual violence, will haunt you long after you close the pages of this book.

In here you will find testimony of justice miscarried, of violence domestic and public, of bigotry and tolerance, of xenophobia and xenophilia. There's too much at stake to shy away from truth, and the writers here have the courage to face it directly, even if the results are brutal. Amid this horror, there is beauty, and a bundle of relationships between aunties, husbands, wives and children, of daughters named 'Hope' and 'Symphony'. All human life is here.

A few visitors have seen this already. Indeed, Kashiefa, Sedick, Zakeer and Sedeeqa Jacobs (page 137) remark on the cottage industry of visitors, students and fellow travellers who had visited – 'Everyday there is people that come from everywhere and ask many questions, then we tell them its not lekker to stay on the road and in the blikkies.' But this book isn't an exercise in prurience. It's a means to dignity, a way for the poor to reflect, be reflected and share with you. This book is testimony to the fact that there's thinking in the shacks, that there are complex human lives and complex humans who dialogue, theorise and fight to bring about change. This book is an expression of that fight, and in reading it, you have been conscripted. *Mon semblable, mon frère*[9] – you are addressed, reader, not as a voyeur, but as a brother or sister, as someone whose eyes dignify the struggle.

If tears fall from your eyes as they did from mine, you will have been touched by the idea, the incredible realisation, that the poor can think for themselves, write for themselves, and will continue to fight for their humanity to be recognised. The residents of Symphony Way have assured us that *a luta continua* – the struggle continues. And they insist that the poor will not be silent when mobs of westerners descend on the so-called 'rainbow nation' to watch football in world-class stadiums. So, whether or not you watched the 2010 World Cup, come to this book with open eyes, and you'll leave with an open heart.

February 2010

Notes

1. United Nations Development Programme (2009) 'Statistics of the Human Development Report', http://hdr.undp.org/en/statistics/, accessed 18 March 2010.
2. Simon Delaney (2007) 'Amandla! Protest in the new South Africa', Freedom of Expression Institute, http://www.fxi.org.za/content/view/83/, accessed 18 March 2010.
3. Richard Pithouse (2009) 'The poor won't go quietly', Times LIVE, 24 November, http://www.timeslive.co.za/opinion/article207581.ece, accessed 18 March 2010.
4. See David Smith (2010) 'Life in "Tin Can Town" for the South Africans evicted ahead of World Cup', *Guardian*, 1 April, http://www.guardian.co.uk/world/2010/apr/01/south-africa-world-cup-blikkiesdorp, accessed 30 June 2010.
5. This ambiguity is being explored by Sharad Chari of the University of KwaZulu Natal and the London School of Economics in his 'Apartheid Remains' project.
6. Mara Kardas-Nelson (2009) 'Eviction threat to refugees', *Mail & Guardian*, 18 March, http://www.mg.co.za/article/2009-03-18-eviction-threat-to-refugees, accessed 18 March 2010.
7. Kennedy Road Development Committee, Abahlali baseMjondolo and the Poor People's Alliance (2009) 'Our movement is under attack', press release, 6 October, http://abahlali.org/node/5860, accessed 18 March 2010.
8. Symphony Way Anti-Eviction Campaign (2009) 'Symphony Way is not dead. We are still Symphony Way. We will always be Symphony Way', press release, Anti-Eviction Campaign Western Cape, 20 October, http://antieviction.org.za/2009/10/30/symphony-way-is-not-dead-we-are-still-symphony-way-we-will-always-be-symphony-way/, accessed 18 March 2010. This press release is reproduced as the Postcript of this book (see page 140).
9. This is a line from the poetry of Charles Baudelaire, whose finger-pointing to the reader was a little more accusatory. Charles Baudelaire, 'Au Lecteur', http://www.press.uchicago.edu/Misc/Chicago/039250.html, accessed 18 March 2010.

Our tap: Symphony Way kids collect water for our families

Introduction

Miloon Kothari

On 10 May 1994, Nelson Rolihlahla Mandela dedicated the day of his inauguration as president of South Africa to 'all the heroes and heroines in this country and the rest of the world who sacrificed in many ways and surrendered their lives so that we could be free … Their dreams have become reality. Freedom is their reward.' He then proclaimed 'Let freedom reign'.[1]

However, in 1999, thousands of desperately poor South Africans (living in government housing, rental units and shacks) began to agitate for a deeper transformation. This was in part a reaction to South Africa's neoliberal economic policy, yet it was also an assertion of dignity and the democratic rights of the poor. Community-based social movements such as the Anti-Eviction Campaign and the Landless People's Movement were born. In 2004, millions of South Africans (44 per cent of the population) abstained from voting in the national election.[2] Many began organising under the banner 'No Land! No House! No Vote!'.[3] Then in 2006, Abahlali baseMjondolo, the South African Shackdwellers' Movement, declared that 27 April was not Freedom Day. They commemorated it as a day of UnFreedom, a day of mourning because they said they lacked toilets, electricity, houses, clinics and libraries. But they also maintain that:

> Freedom is more than all of this. Freedom is a way of living not a list of demands to be met. Delivering houses will do away with the lack of houses but it won't make us free on its own. Freedom is a way of living where everyone is important and where everyone's experience and intelligence counts … We have often said that we are not free because even many of the people who say that they are for the struggles of the poor refuse to accept that we can think for ourselves.[4]

The Symphony Way Pavement Dwellers' struggle for dignity is expressed through the content of this anthology and the process by which they wrote it. While making lists of material demands such as housing, residents also give scorching indictments of government oppression and corruption. They are quite clear that their struggle is for both basic needs and sociopolitical freedom.

One of the community leaders said on the eve of their occupation of Symphony Way: 'We may be poor but we are not stupid! We may be poor, but we can still think!' Each story, then, can be seen as affirmation by the residents of their intelligence and expertise in their own struggle. Through this struggle, they have learned to respect themselves, to respect their ideas and to respect their distinct vernacular.

When the Symphony Way residents discussed in mass meetings how they would go about writing this book, they came to a consensus that the book should be written in their own language. They were quite clear in their insistence that, with a couple of exceptions, they did not speak the 'Queen's English' nor did they ever learn to speak formal Afrikaans. Therefore, how could their stories be presented in anything but their very own Cape Flats slang?

Through dialogue, the residents also came to a consensus that the book would be written, first and foremost, for themselves. While they were hoping that in writing this book the world could hear about their lives, their dreams and their struggles, they were also adamant that they were writing a history that they and their families would be able to cherish forever.

Having an outsider editing these stories would have destroyed the most precious attribute of this anthology: its authenticity.

Voices from Symphony Way is radical because it destroys the myth of the 'ignorance of the poor'. It challenges the assertion that there is only one genuine way to speak or write a language. It turns the industrial complex surrounding the production of knowledge on its head.

As a participatory project of the community, the residents set about to further demand that anyone seeking to publish this anthology adhere to a few other conditions:

- That each completed story be included within the book. That no publisher was permitted to remove any story even if some of them were considered by their professional authority to be too short, somewhat redundant, difficult to read or unmarketable.
- That all promotion of the book be done in consultation with the community.
- That each family receive at least one copy of the book once it is published.
- And that proceeds (if any) from the book go collectively to the community.

The community felt that using these rules as a starting point in negotiations with a publisher was the only way to make sure that ownership of the project remained in their hands and that the story, in its raw and real form, would be told in its entirety.

Because of this, each and every story weaves together as a work of art that contributes to a culture of plurality and resistance from within a collective community consciousness.

So, as the struggle on Symphony Way is a radically democratic one, *Voices from Symphony Way* takes that struggle to the powers that be in the publishing industry by saying: how dare you confine us within your narrow world of profit and cultural elitism. We are not *dom*.[5] We demand you open up. We demand you listen to our words. We demand our freedom. We count too.

***

When I conducted a mission for the United Nations to South Africa in 2007 I was deeply moved by the struggle, fortitude and courage of the groups I met – the Anti-Eviction Campaign, the Landless People's Movement and Abahlali baseMjondolo. I was impressed with the intense process of human rights education and learning these communities had gone through. I was inspired by the manner in which the communities were claiming their human rights, including the right to adequate housing, and the awareness they exhibited as to how these claims were rooted in their own dignity, in the South African constitution and in the international human rights instruments.

During the mission and the visit to different communities, I was disturbed to learn and to see that their genuine voices were not only not acknowledged by the authorities but that there was open hostility towards the legitimate, human-rights-based demands articulated by these voices. I called, in my mission report, for there to be dialogue between the communities and the state and the creation of a permanent space for the participation of these communities in all planning processes that affect their lives.[6]

***

The arrangement of the stories

In keeping with the authors' desire to give readers an authentic peek into their community, there is no thematic order to this collection of stories. Instead, they are arranged according to where their authors lived on the road – the first story being situated at the northern end and the last story at the southern end of the settlement (see the map of Symphony Way on p. 6). While thematically and chronologically random, this placement helps give readers a geographic understanding of the settlement while also expressing the diversity of views and opinions among residents.

The numbers that precede each person's/family's name is the informal house number (as opposed to the unused and inaccurate formal house numbers that were forcibly sprayed onto the hokkies by City officials). One can tell a lot about the settlement and the community's struggle for houses just by looking at and

Daddycare

analysing these numbers. Many families, for instance, chose for various reasons not to submit their own stories. Yet, one thing that should not be assumed is that the 90 independent structures correspond to 90 families living on the road. Instead, there were many families that shared structures because they were either related to one another or close friends.

Government policy must learn from and be based on the demands, needs, human rights and grassroots knowledge of those who are most vulnerable. The courageous voices in this book bear testimony to the adverse and completely unacceptable conditions in which these communities are forced to exist. Real credibility, at home and abroad, for the South African state will only come if it heeds the call for radical change emanating from the eloquent voices presented in this book.

Miloon Kothari is the former Special Rapporteur on Adequate Housing, UN Human Rights Council and coordinator of the South Asia Regional Programme of the Housing and Land Rights Network

New Delhi, India

July 2010

4

Notes

1. Statement of the president of the African National Congress, Nelson Rolihlahla Mandela, at his inauguration as president of the democratic Republic of South Africa, Union Buildings, Pretoria on 10 May 1994, http://www.anc.org.za/ancdocs/history/mandela/1994/inaugpta.html, accessed 18 March 2010.
2. Eunice Ajambo (2006) 'Inaction as action: South Africa's political culture of protest and the declining voter turnout', http://www.people.carleton.edu/~amontero/Eunice%20Ajambo.pdf, accessed 18 March 2010.
3. Richard Pithouse (2005) '"No vote" campaigns are not a rejection of democracy', *Mail and Guardian*, November, http://www.abahlali.org/node/865, accessed 18 March 2010.
4. Abahlali baseMjondolo (2008) 'Abahlali baseMjondolo to mourn UnFreedom Day once again', 21 April 2008, http://www.abahlali.org/node/3480, accessed 18 March 2010.
5. 'Dom' is a widely used South African slang term, originating from Afrikaans, which translates as 'dumb' or 'stupid'.
6. See Miloon Kothari (2008) 'Report of the Special Rapporteur on Adequate Housing: Mission to South Africa', UN Doc. No. A/HRC/7/16/Add.3, 29 February, http://www2.ohchr.org/english/issues/housing/visits.htm, accessed 23 August 2010.

All in a day's work: overhauling the family car on the pavement

The Road (aka Symphony Way), looking towards the southeast

The above photograph was taken a few steps towards the southeast from community-initiated roadblock number 1

City-initiated roadblock number 1

The beginning of shacks, part of the Symphony Way Pavement Dweller Community

First story by the Williams family takes place here

The N2 Gateway houses that were occupied by Delft Backyard Dwellers in December 2007

Community-initiated roadblock number 1

Community-initiated roadblock number 2

Symphony Way Anti-Eviction Campaign Office, Community Centre and Creche

Community-initiated roadblock number 3

Aunty Jane Roberts' story takes place here by the office

Final story by Kashiefa Jacobs takes place here

City-intiated roadblock number 2

This is the land where the Symphony Way TRA (aka Blikkiesdorp) was built by the City of Cape Town

Tsunami Temporary Relocation Area, part of the N2 Gateway Housing Project

This is the hard truth...

THIS IS THE hard truth being lived by human beings, even animals live a better life, so to read this book will help you one day when it happens to you because no one knows the future...

The Poor People give us the mandate to fight for their rights and we try to give them positive feedback to fight for this mandate. That is our type of people's government here on the road and the whole Anti-Eviction Campaign communities. People are deciding on their own destiny. The People decide, not me or Jerome or the Anti-Eviction.

We, the Western Cape Anti-Eviction Campaign, stands for the less fortunate and also for what is ritefully deprived to the poor – the right not to be silent from broken promises of government. That is why we are Independent from political parties. We expose corruption from *High People* like Government. We do the illegal to expose the corruption of the legal, that is the philosophy of our activism.

Truth is not easy to accept so it is essential to learn better-ways to help the Poor from suffering and to stop corruption. We stand firm for what is Right and to stop the Rich from stealing from the Poor. But teach them 'the Rich' to share. For now it is about a house thing and the struggle continues because its not only about houses. That is why the struggle will always continue until corruption stop and so that people can live a better life and be treated like citizens of South Africa.

You know the rights of the people and when you expose something, you want people to know what they stand for.

We teach Poor People to Stand Together and to stand for what is right – that's what makes us unique.

Chapter 1

Since 1984 I started working at a clothing factory. In the next year the workers selected me as a shop-steward. The shop-steward represents workers in all matters relating to the company they work for. Then I became a fulltime shop-steward for the South African Clothing and Textile Union (SACTU). A fulltime shop-steward recruits people from different factories. When the workers at a company doesn't belong to a union, I would go and recruit the workers. When I was working as a fulltime shop-steward at SACTU, when COSATU [Congress of South African Trade Unions] had meetings, then I must attend COSATU meetings because COSATU is the umbrella for all the anti-Apartheid unions. I was still working at COSATU and SACTU while also working in the communities as *troublemaker* against Apartheid.

Chapter 2

Back then, I was still a supporter of the ANC [African National Congress] and the United Democratic Front. I was also part of the Valhalla Park Civic since 1984. If theres water cuts, we put the water back on. If theres evictions, we put the people back into their houses. There was a lot of movements in Valhalla park whose doing the same things. Then we go to have a meeting with all these movements and then we asked them *why can't we come together and be one*. And then we started the UnitedFront around 1986. The UnitedFront stood for no evictions, no water-cuts, scrapping arrears, upgrades of sports fields.

Chapter 3

In the old Apartheid, they evicted people, they cut off electricity, and people was living in the squatter camps. Now, since 1994, we having a new ANC government. The only thing did change is that now I can go anywhere or live anywhere if I have money. Otherwise, for me, its the same government, but only different faces. Because why? There's still evictions, there's still water cuts, there's still no scrapping of arrears. We are fighting for a government that listens to the poor people, not to rich people. Mandela didn't solve all the problems. Change is only possible only if the ordinary people have a say in problems.

Chapter 4

In other communities the same thing happened where people's lights and water were put off, and where they were evicted, places like Tafelsig and more places. They were doing the same work. We knew there was people in Tafelsig and the whole Mitchell's Plain. We just hear that they was doing the same thing but we never met them as a committee.

In 2000 we met Ashraf Cassiem. There was a committee similar to our United-Front in Tafelsig. Our first meeting we had in Valhalla Park with the committee of Tafelsig. Then after that, we had a discussion and we said, OK, let we come together, because why? We are doing the same thing. In the same year we launch the Western Cape Anti-Eviction Campaign in Tafelsig.

Chapter 5

I was still in the union in 2001 and I decided to leave and come and work in the community fulltime. Because why? I did see what happen in COSATU. They having meetings, they having congress of the unions. And there they adopted a policy: *Housing Crisis*. And they spoke about it but nothing happened in the communities. When COSATU say something they don't do it because they are in alliance with the ANC and they can't fight the government because of the alliance. I think that if COSATU wants to be a proper union and fighting for poor people or workers, or whatever, then they must broke the alliance. Then they got more power to put pressure on the government.

It was better to work in the community because if you work in the community and don't belong to a COSATU in alliance with the ANC, then you can do more things, fight for people against evictions and many other problems.

Chapter 6

The 25th of October 2002 I moved out of Valhalla Park to Delft, because, why? I did get an RDP house[1] here in Delft, Leiden. The same year the same evictions happened in Delft. In 2003 we launch the Delft Anti-Eviction Campaign as a committee. We started helping the people in Delft because evictions and water-cuts started in Delft. We did having the youth to motivate: we started netball, football and church programs.

Chapter 7

The people always went to the councillor (Frank Martin) to find out when they were going to get their houses. In 2007 Frank Martin started organising meetings for houses for the people. The 16th of December Frank Martin handed out the first illegal copies of the houses. The 17th of December Frank Martin the councillor let people occupy houses illegaly at the N2 Gateway housing project. And

Youngsters of Symphony Way played ball games yesterday, spending Freedom Day in a different way. PICTURE: CINDY WAXA

Homeless mark 'un-Freedom Day'

NOMANGESI MBIZA
Staff Reporter

AS SOUTH Africans celebrated 15 years of democracy, the pavement dwellers of Symphony Way marked what they termed "un-Freedom Day".

The families, facing eviction from the pavement they decided to occupy more than a year ago after being kicked out of newly-built houses destined for other families, yesterday hosted visitors from other informal settlements in Khayelitsha and Philippi, along with backyard dwellers from Guguletu.

"We decided to host this event because people say we are free, while we are not. If we are free, why are we living on a road and some people in shacks in informal settlements?" questioned Anti-Eviction Campaign spokeswoman Jane Roberts.

The small community of 127 families held a series of sporting events, and put on plays which reflected their lives.

"We have a netball team, and football teams here. We invited other teams from around Delft to come and play here," Roberts said.

"The children put on a play which showed what happened when we were evicted from the houses, and when police came here to give us court orders."

She said she was happy to see the children who live in Symphony Way having a day of play, just like normal children.

"It was nice seeing children playing and enjoying themselves."

Aphiwe Mlandu, of Site B in Khayelitsha, said she decided to join the activities, because she too was not free.

"I might not be staying on a pavement, but I am in the same situation as the people of Symphony Way because I also live in a shack," she said.

"The rain started last week already and we are living in fear. Some of us will have to leave our homes and stay with relatives for the rest of winter," she said.

nomangesi.mbiza@inl.co.za

on the 19th of December Frank Martin the councillor was the chairperson in the meeting and he handed illegal copies to two hundred extra people for houses. After the other two hundred people, he said to the other people he didn't have the illegal copies for the houses, they can occupied the house they like. So they moved in the houses. The Delft Anti-Eviction Campaign committee was in the meetings. I knew it was wrong for the councillor to tell the people to move in the houses. I knew that would cause trouble, that's why I attended the meetings and tried to stop Frank Martin. He don't want to listen, he just went on and the people occupied the houses.

Chapter 8

The first eviction was on the 21st December with an illegal court order. Frank Martin wasn't there, he was in his office. So I told the Western Cape chairperson because I know this was the start of big trouble. The Delft Anti-Eviction Campaign and the Western Cape Anti-Eviction Campaign came together and on the same day we went to court and we stopped the eviction. Because why? The eviction order was illegal.

Also, if you listen to the people, they was waiting so long on the waiting for houses (some was 20 years, 15 years), thats why we wanted to stop the eviction to help those people stay in the houses. There was a lot of corruption on housing which meant that the right people were not getting houses. The backlog is over 400,000 and its not enough houses being built for people. We supported them because why? They was backyard dwellers in Delft who was poor and occupied the houses, and they were making a statement that the N2 Gateway was a failed project and the N2 Gateway didn't make the backlog less than it is. I am going to add Joe Slovo [Informal Settlement] also into this thing, because why? Resistance to the N2 Gateway was also started by Joe Slovo because of the government wanting to relocate them to Delft. The people in Delft that occupied these houses were misinformed about the whole allocation process. They thought that the people of Joe Slovo were getting these houses but in the meantime those people were relocated to TRAs [Temporary Relocation Areas].

We supported these people, the occupiers of the N2 Gateway because they got nowhere to go and they were pushed into a corner from Frank Martin.

Chapter 9

I feel happy that there is going to be a book so that other people can read about the struggle of Symphony Way. This book is going to be a true reflection of how people feel about their own struggle. These stories will tell you more about how people feel and the history of Symphony Way as a powerful and motivated community that stands together.

We stand together as a community and do what is right.

To everyone in the struggle, to anyone who is reading this book: *let your voice be heard to stop broken promises from corrupted government. Speaking is the struggle to freedom.*

Aluta Continua!

From: Jane Roberts (Chairperson)
Delft Anti-Eviction Campaign

Note

1. The houses built by the new government after 1994 under the Reconstruction and Development Programme. Although the programme was soon replaced by another, the RPD name stuck.

Camaraderie

Carpet out to dry

Eviction

ON THE 19TH FEBRUARY was the day of hell.

It was 6 o'clock in the morning when my neighbour shouted: *here's the police coming.* We were one of the first families who'se stuff was taken. People had to hurry up to get there things, if they did not hurry up a big truck would pick up your stuff. And you would not get them back. While my husband was busy taking our stuff out of the house, I was in the street already changing my baby's nappy. That was when they started to load our stuff on the truck. There was a bag with my husband's medicine in on the truck. I asked one of the guys that came with the trucks for the bag and he did not want to gave it so we started to argue. While I was busy with him, two of the other guys lifted my baby's pram with the baby in it on the truck. I told them that my baby was in the pram and that they can't put the pram on the truck. My husband had to fought with them because they just wanted to give the baby but they wanted to keep the pram on the truck. I lost everything, they even took my baby's cloths, the kimbies [disposable nappies], everything. My furniture, food, they just took everything.

The one thing I will never forget is this one particular guy. I remember asking one of the police guys for a blanket to cover my baby on the pram – and he refused. He said, *why must I give you the blanket, it is not my child. You know you were supposed to be out*. She was only a month old. The police did not feel a thing when they evict us. They shot at us and they did not care if there were children. Children were crying being afraid. The police were very rude. All they wanted to do was to shoot at us.

We were afraid and did not know where to go. We desided to move on to the pavement and we did not have any structure. The first night we slept in the open air. That night my neighbor who I did not even know at the time, offered me a blanket to throw over the pram. Even though the policeman didn't feel a thing for my baby, a poor person with nothing did. I lost my trust in the police that day.

My Shack were one of the first Shacks that were build. The police came and threw the shack down but we just rebuild it. We stayed on the pavement and people came to look at us and the newspaper came every morning to take Photos. We felt humiliated. You see, there was people that was making fun of us. They said things like: *you know you was not supposed to move in and now you are on the street like dogs*.

At that time, I was very afraid, but now, I feel much stronger. I will do it again. If it is the only way of putting a roof over my children's heads, I will do it again.

Many things had happen since the eviction, some was good and some was bad but all I think of is the day the words come '*Here is your keys*', that is the words I've been waiting for.

Anthea and Theodore Williams and family

The Bush of Evil

I NEVER THOUGHT that December 2007 last year would be like a death sentence. And maybe if I knew that October 2008 would be *hell*, then maybe I wouldn't have moved into the houses in the first place.

When thousands of families including myself moved into these houses we never thought that we would be treated like animals. We went to court almost everyday having the hope that we would get those houses. We thought that we had a right to have a house. I thought that my children deserved to be able to say that they have a house and a roof over their heads. To be able to stay at one place for more than a month or year. *To be able to call it their own*.

The 19th of February was a scary day for all of us. We were evicted from the houses that my children called a home. The morning of the 19th we got a knock on the door telling me that the police had come with Army trucks. So my children wake up and came outside to see all those police. People were scared

and children were crying. We started packing our stuff. Waiting and praying that the appeal of the court is threw. While waiting the police came and threw our stuff from the houses. With these big guns not caring that our children is there. If you did not take your stuff then they would put it on a truck and you would not get it back. We carried our stuff on the other side of the houses on the road. We carried our stuff in a hurry. I remember that there was a moment when someone told that the appeal were threw and all of the people were happy. I got this feeling of joy knowing that know my children has a house now. After a few minutes it came like my heart were ripped from my chest when they told us it was not for us. Our family were not prepared for that. We had nowhere else to go so we moved to the pavement. We had no structures to build a shack. So we took our bed and our other things and made a structure. The newspaper people came every morning to take pictures. We got donations of food and clothing. People were not prepared for any of these. We had marches to different places. We thought that we would get houses with in a month. Then in about the middle of the year.

We had people robbing our own people in their Shacks because they didn't know each other and they had lost their jobs. In the beginning it was very dangerous because it was different families coming from different places. There were one incident when someone from outside the community wanted to rape one of the young girls but did not get it right. The girl ran home and told her mother. One night, we was sleeping, and then we heard screeming and got up and then we saw a big fire not knowing where it came from. When we could see where it came from, 4 Shacks we burning out, but no one did no how the fire got started. The 4 families lost everything exept their lives.

But then people start to know each other and love each other. We began to talk. It didn't matter if we were of a different religion or culture, we understood each other because we were all for one thing – for houses. It became a lot safer on the road. Or so we thought.

The worst of it all was that were we lived in Symphony Way there were a bush behind us. This is Nikita, my daughter's, story of the bush of evil and the day of evil.

'The *Bush of Evil*: The a place where many things has happened and where a lot of people has gotten hurt. For example, one night while we were sleeping we heard a voice of a woman screeming help! Help! All of our people ran to go and see. When we got there it was an African women from outside the community screeming because her boyfriend had beaten her. There was people going in and out of the bush looking for him.

October 1st was the worst day of all. Many people would write about that day but no one had ouir feeling and knowledge of that day. It was the biggest day for our Moslems, it was what we call as Eid, because it is almost like Christmas. On that day my sister decided to go to the bush as she went almost everyday. She loved the bush. My mother did not want her to go there but she went anyway not hearing for my mother. On that day she and 3 of her friends had gone to the bush but what was scary is the fact that I should have gone with but by some mircale I was busy. When I got home I saw her shoes lying on the ground and thought to myself *how could she have gone with out me?* I was angry at her. I wanted to go to sleep because I was tired and angry with her. The one of the ladys called 'here comes Wadia them'. So I stand up to see what was going on. My sister, as well as her friends, came and she was crying and a boy that was with them was also naked. Then she told us the story about what had happened. We all started crying. My mom ran to the bush and looked but saw no one. That was there worst day ever.

That is my daughter's story of the bush of evil. The day before was my late husband's birthday so it was already a sad day. On the 1st of October, when my child came crying and running from the bush she told me the worst thing a mother could ever imagen. Is the words 'mommy he broke my virgin'. These were the worst words ever. I did not know what to do I just ran into the bush and went looking for the Guy. People came and all did cry. I as a mother I felt so Guilty because I could not protect my daughter. The she ask me 'mommy what did I do wrong. Why did it happen to me? I asked Allah to protect me and he didn't do it'. So I told her, 'You never asked for it and so you did nothing wrong. This is a man who did this, don't blame religion for this. Allah did protect you, because she came home alive.'

We went looking everyday for about a week for the Guy; we did not catch him. Not yet…but I then told my daughter that we should leave it in Allah's hands because what he did to you, he is going to get it worse.

I see the fear everyday in my child's eyes knowing that my child had to see another man on her body. Everyday is a struggle. We don't know what happen. We don't when we get houses or things like this might happen again. But we continue to pray and fight. We mustn't stop fighting for our kids sakes. We will get houses!

Lola Wentzel and family

Court case of two innocent people

TWO OF OUR very well known people, who was doing their best to help us to get houses who had families of their own and only wanted the best for them. They had help our community.

On that night of April 2008, two of the shacks were throwed down and people were mad. The people were mad because Brother John and Elmarie [former residents on the road] were backstabbers. Brother John and Elmarie went behind the people's backs of Symphony. They did their own thing, trying to influence people to go against the AEC [Anti-Eviction Campaign] committee while they themselves were on the committee. They didn't work with the community, they worked against the community.

The people of Symphony were cross, so they wanted them off the road. There is no place on Symphony for traitors. So they throwed down the shacks to get rid of them.

The woman, Elmarie, of the one shack who was throw down was very angry. An The man of the other shack brough his sons. They came with pangas

[machetes] and with a gun and started shooting at our people. One of the woman almost got shot, and one of the men throw himself upon her, and got shot in his foot. That was Brother Ryan Jackson. He was a brave man because he saved that woman's life. We phone the cops, but they just past by.

And that same night they arrested Jerome & Riedwaan. The lady, Elmarie, laid a charge against them, saying they had broke her shack down. But Jerome and Wannie wasn't involved. Riedwaan wasn't even there on the road at the time. Jerome wasnt involved in the incident at all.

Everybody on the road went down to the police station and stayed there the whole night till 3 in the morning. Ashraf and the committee went into the charge office and went to find out whats going to happen to Jerome and Wannie. And when they came out they told the residents of Symphony to go back home. That the police were going to keep them in custody.

They got 12 months sentence for breaking down the shacks. Jerome and Riedwaan got sent to different prisons. Jerome came out of jail within a few months. Jerome got out on the 2nd of October. And Riedwaan a few days after that.

I was cross and upset because I felt it was wrong. They did nothing wrong. I dont know why got punished for something they did not do.

Your Sincerely
Jolene Arendse

Untitled

IN DECEMBER 2007 I move into a house in N2 Gateway, Symphony Way, Delft. I always thought that the house will be mine.

On February 19, I was evict from that house. I wake up at 5:30am to see the hole street full of police, trucks, people and more police. We did have a big fight that day. The police did put other people furniture on the trucks. They used foreigners to do their dirty work. When it was my turn in the afternoon my things were already in Symphony Way.

In anycase the police makes a huge shooting between the people that was evicted from the houses. We were fighting with them. Rubber bullets were hurting the people. Two of my friends were hit. One on the back and the other on the leg.

My one friend who was shot in the leg's name is Heraldine. We grew up together in Bishop Lavis [a township in Cape Town]. We attended the same high school. I was angry when I saw that she had been hit by a rubber bullet. I took her into one of the houses that we were evicted from and she show me where the bullet hit. I took her outside again and told her that Jared is taking pictures of all the injured people and that she must also go. After the pictures where taken she went to the hospital. The other friend of mine is just somebody I met while we were still living in the houses.

They almost shot me but a fall let the bullet passes me.

I am still in Symphony Way, in the struggle of getting my house I can call home. I will stay here until I get what I need. And what I Zuleiga Dyers needs is a house to call my own.

From,
Zuleiga Dyers
Delft Symphony
Thanks a lot

You can still get married on the pavement

MY NAME IS Qiyaamudeen Alexander; I am a 31 year old man living on the pavement of Symphony Way, Delft with my 20 year old wife Kashiefa Alexander. We occupied the house illegaly in N2 Gateway with my mother-in-law Shamiela Fataar. We were evicted like animals by the police on the 19 February 2008.

While we occupied the houses we made plans to get married on the Sunday 16 March 2008; But everything changed and we cancelled everything; Because we thought we couldn't get married on the pavement. We felt hopeless and lost and we thought nothing would work for us. I lost my job at the bakery in Houtbay; Because of staying out of work. Everything was new for me because I used to live in Kensington, It was difficult to travel from Delft to Houtbay. Travelling allowance was 1,000 Rand and wages was only 2,000 Rand. I had to wake up 4 o'clock to start travelling by quarter past 5 to get there at 7 o'clock.

Because of our situation our hope for getting married was lost. At least we thought so; Because as we started knowing our neighbours; we learned how we could help and support each other. We started knowing what each other's problems were and we started feeling like we wanted to be like a family. They said, *no man, you can still get married on the pavement, its not something to be embarrased about.* That was when we decided on a date for our big day. Our next door neighbour offered me a job with him and we went to work in Melkbosstrand where we did the plumbing and tiling at a house which lasted for a month in which we could save money for everything we needed. At first we decided to have a big ceremony, but we then changed our minds and decided to have something small and simple.

When I met Kashiefa I was a christian and my name was Quinton and I had to change my name and religion before we got married. The reason why I wanted to change my religion is because I admire the way Muslim's live and how they live out of their faith. How they stick to each other and help each other. On the 27 March 2008 I imbraced the Muslim Deen [faith] and the Imaam who help me achieve that was Imaam Samarudeen Stemmet whose family lives on the road with us; May Allah grant him and his family their health and everything that is beautiful in the Deen Insha-Allah [God willing]. After that with the help of our neighbours we planned our big day. The Symphony Way committee offered the community office space for the ceremony. With the help of neighbours, my wife to be ordered the dresses; cakes and booked the photographer. A friend of ours offered us as a wedding gift a house which we could use as our honeymoon suit for 2 weeks.

When the big day finally arrived we were nervous and excited. I woke up the morning at 8am very excited and couldn't wait to get married. I didn't know what to expect. I was away from my wife to-be for two weeks – that is the way we are supposed to be in the Muslim religion. That makes the love and the way I missed her grow stronger. While I was preparing myself, my wife to be and family and friends was busy preparing everything at home like decorating the office and the house; fetching the cakes and getting dressed. Imaam Samarudeen Stemmet was the Imaam who performed the marriage ceremony. When I got to the mosque, I didn't know what to expect. It was my first time at an actual mosque and I didn't prepare myself for what to expect. At that time only, then the Imaam explained to me what to do. He would pray in arabic language and I would just have to listen. I had to confess and say that I accept my wife Kashiefa with all the responsibilities that come with it. I got married at Belhar Mosque at 13h40 and my wife was waiting for me at home.

From the mosque I went home to my wife where I was welcomed by family and friends and neighbours and my beautiful wife. We took photos, was greeted by everyone and from home we went to the office where we celebrated our big day with family and friends. That was the happiest day of our time on the pavement in Symphony Way, Delft. From there we went to our honeymoon suit which was beautifully decorated by our friends for us to enjoy. The Saturday 26 April 2008 is a day we will never forget.

Firstly we want to thank Ashraf Cassiem for everything that he is doing to help us in this struggle for houses. May Allah grant him and his family their health and reward all abundantly; 'Ameen'. Then we want to thank the following people: my mother Lorraine Alexander; Mother-in-law Shamielah Fataar; sincere friends Imaam Samarudeen Stemmet and his wife Mastoera Stemmet, Boeta Qiyaamudeen and wife Moemiena; neighbours Auntie Rashieda, Auntie Jane and Auntie Badru and all our other friends and neighbours for their support, may the almighty Allah reward all abundantly Insha-Allah, Ameen.

Now our struggle goes on and we are still on the pavement and my wife is now 6 months pregnant and we endure all this cold; wet; hot; dry and sandy weather. The struggle made me a new person in the way of my self-confidence. At first I was only a person where if something failed the first time, I would give up hope. But here on the struggle, I learned how to keep on trying and motivating myself. By the end you will be victorious.

Being married is like something new for me, now that I am married, I have something to fight for. Fight for houses and fight for my family. Because if I wasn't married, I would have given up hope long ago and I would have told myself I don't have anything to fight for. The year 2008 is almost at an end and we're still struggling for houses. We're praying that good news will come our way soon.

Qiyaamudeen Alexander

Geagte Lesers

EK WIL U graag deel hoe die Madrassa ontstaan het. Ons was ge-evict op die 19 Febuarie 2008 uit die huise.ons het hier op die pavement in Symphony Way ons tuise gemaak. Dit was vir ons baie swaar om aan te pas hier. Ek was baie hatseer want dit is nie die lewe wat ek ken nie, en wat ek vir my kinders wil hê nie, maar omdat ek geen ander plek gehad het nie, en weer terug in ander mense agterplaas wil bly nie, moes ek ook maar hier deur byt. Dinge het baie swaar gegaan, want ons het ons werke verloor.

Ek dink die rede dat ek hier nog sit is oor my sterk believe in my creator en omdat ek so baie dink aan die kinders wat ook graag 'n huis will hê dat ek nog vandag nog hier is. Ek het baie dinge geleer hier op die pavement. Ek het met different mense gewoon en ook gelewe. Die mense het begin in verkeerde rigtinge gelewe, die kinders het uit die skole gegaan, elkeen was besig met sy eie lewe, en daar was niks beheer oor die kinders nie, dinge het woes gegaan. Ek het besluit dinge kan nie so aan gaan nie, en gedink aan my familie en ook ander kinders, so ek moet iets doen. Een aand was hier 'n meeting hier in die pad, ek het gegaan en 'n voorstel gemaak om 'n Madrassa vir moslem kinders te hou. Ons leader wat behoort aan die enti-eviction, Ashraf Cassiem, het die meeting gehou en ek het die voorstel aan hom gesê, hy het dit in die meeting gekondig dat die ouers moet hulle kinders stuur. Die kinders het nie gekom nie, ek het besluit om na elke hok te gaan en die kinders aan te moedig.

In April het die Madrassa begin met net nege kinders. Die nege kinders was baie gewillig om te leer. Hulle het in die oggend 6 o'clock, wanneer dit ons prayer time is, gekom bid. Hulle het die dag begin, en so het dit hulle opgebou in geloof. Elke middag na skool het hulle kom leer en ook praying time, want ons moet 5 keer 'n dag pray. In die Madrassa was hier net twee kinders wat in die Koeraan was, die ander was almal beginners. Ek het weer eens gegaan en die ander kinders gaan aanmoedig, en ons het nou 32 kinders. Daar was tye wat ek ongeduldig geraak het, want som ouers het nie hulle samewerking gegee nie, maar ek het deur gedruk deur die krag van my Creator. Ek voel trots dat ons so sterk staan op 32 kinders. Ons het nou 8 kinders wat nou in die Koeraan is, en ek glo die anders gaan ook daar bo uit kom. Ons is so gebless met die Madrassa dat ons help gekry het wat vir ons Koeraane en ook prayer matte gebring het. En nou kry ons ook almal op die pavement Sondae kos. Ons het nou ons Children's Day gehad op die 4 Desember 2008, die Children's Day was 'n groot sukses. Die mense wat gehoor het van die Madrassa hier op Symphony Way het ook vir die kinders certificates uit gegee.

Ek bedank ook almal vir hulle bystand. Ek moet sê as jy jou trust in jou Creator sit sal jy altyd bo uit kom. Ek glo ook hierdie kinders gaan dit ver bring as hulle so aan hou, en ook hulle familie. Mag hierdie Madrassa gaan van sterkte tot sterkte. Met die krag van ons Creator gaan die Madrassa volgende jaar nog meerder kinders wees.

To make a success of something is to believe and put your trust in your Creator.

R. Levember

Dear Reader

I JUST WANT to share with you how the Madrassa [Islamic school] started out. We were evicted on 19 February 2008 and we just end up on the pavement in Symphony Way out of these houses. It was very difficult to adapt here. I was so heart-sore because that is not the life I know, and this is not what I would like for my kids, because I don't have another place to stay, and I can't go back to the backyards where I stayed before. I had to compromise a lot of things because we lost our jobs.

The reason why I am still on the road is because I am a strong believer in my creator and I think a lot about the children that need homes and that are still staying here. On the pavement I have learned a lot of things and even to communicate with people. People started going the wrong direction and children stayed out of school. Everyone was busy with their own lives and there was no control over the children. So I just decided that things can't go on like that, so I have to do something about it. One evening, there was a meeting, I went and I made a suggestion that we have to open a Madrassa for the moslem kids. Our leader in that meeting and our chairperson, Ashraf Cassiem, announced my suggestion that the parents must send their children to the Madrassa. I decided to go to each and every shack to motivate the parents and the children.

In April, the Madrassa started with only 9 children. These 9 children were

Learning at the Symphony Way Madrassa

very willing to learn. They even came at 6 o'clock in the morning for our [the parents'] prayer time. When they are starting their day, spiritually they are build themselves in prayer. We pray five times a day and every afternoon the school children come and learn. By the Madrassa, there were only two children who knew the Koran and the others were all beginners. I went back again to go and motivate more children and now there are 32 children in the Madrassa. There were times that I was unhappy because some parents didn't give their effort, but I pulled through through the strength of my Creator. I'm proud that we are so strong with the 32 children. From two, there are now 8 children who know the Koran and I believe the rest will also succeed. We are so blessed by the Madrassa that we got help of gifts of Korans and the prayer carpets. And we, the pavement dwellers, all receive food on Sundays. We had Children's Day the 4th of December 2008, the children's day was a big success. The people that heard about the Madrassa on Symphony way, issued out certificates to our kids.

I thank all that stood by me. I must say that if you trust in your Creator, everything will be successful. I believe that the children will uphold it [the teachings of the Madrassa] share what they are doing with their families. May this Madrassa grow stronger and stronger. With the strength of the Creator this Madrassa will be still here next year and with more children.

To make a success of something is to believe and put your trust in your Creator.

R. Levember

To the minister of housing

THE REASON WHY I need a house is I am a 46 year old woman, I have 3 children, and I am a single mother. I am 20 years on the waiting list. In the past I was live by my sister in Kensington but that was my mothers house. After that, my mother passed away and then the house go over to my older sister. The reason why the house go over to my older sister is because I was married and my husband was the one who was to go to the City and inquire for a house. He passed away in 1994, the same year as Shakira, my daughter, was born. Every time when I go there by the City of Cape Town and ask about my house, they say there is no house. And that was the reason why I come to Delft-Symphony Way.

I am here for a year and two months and on the struggle on the street. I got ill on the street. I am sick woman, I have epilepsy and arthritis and high blood. This effect me a lot. I go for my treatment and my tablets and injections at Sumerset Hospital. I am working for my 3 children. Sometimes I have to struggle for food but why do I need to struggle for a house. A house is for free for everyone.

Everybody must get a house. But why do I have to struggle alone with my children. My one child has asma because of struggling on the road for a house. This is not only for me but for my children. When I pass away then I know my kids is under a roof. Sometimes when its raining, then it is leaking through my hokkie [shack]. Then my house is wet. My beds is getting wet and it is very cold in here. That is the reason we must make a fire to keep us warm.

Ek et nie geweetan struggle nie. *I didnt know the struggle*. The reason why I am staying here is that I can feel that I grow up stronger. All the people on this road is not rude with me. We are a happy family here. They support me and is good for me.

The struggle for me is now, we all together standing together and if something happens then we all standing together. Even when the cops come here and try and chase us away, we stand together.

The reason I was stay for a long time in hokkies, and that is the reason I want now a house, is so I can feel that I am a mother of the house. I am sick and tired of staying in a hok'.

The struggle has open my mind and open my eyes. You can see what is going on. I know that struggle now because we know we go to the court the 9th of June and we know that the prosecutor can send us to Blikkiesdorp and we don't want to go to Blikkiesdorp. A lot of things go on there in Blikkiesdorp.

From
Shamiela Fataar

The fire and the struggle on Symphony Rd

IT WAS A very sad day. My whole family and 3 children was crying. We really thought that we are going to get the houses. That same night we move to the pavement with the other families, but me and the children didn't get sleep on the pavement that night. We slept by my brother in Leiden because my baby was only 2 weeks old. My husband build a shack for us. We didn't have any material and he had to go look for material, knock on people's door. Sometimes he would come with nothing and then we have to use a sail instead of a door. But the next day he would go again and look and find something for us. It took us a week to build the shack how we want it. We had to fit in because it was a new experience.

On the 15th May 2008 our shack burn to the ground. We were sleeping and it was like someone woke me up. As I turn I just saw flames. I got such afraid. I was screaming for my family. I grab the baby and my husband took the 2 girls.

We were so lucky. We lost everything, but that is nothing compare to our lives. We thank God for sparing our lives.

We don't really actually know how the fire started. At first we thought it started by our shack. But then afterwards there was so lot of stories on the road. People would come and ask where we saw the flames. They would say no, this is impossible, someone did put something in the back and did start the fire. I'm not one to think someone would do something like that to us. After the stories, I just put it out of my head and me and my families just moved on because I don't want to blame anyone. I'm already so grateful that me and my family is still alive. If anyone should get the blame, it is the government. Its that Judge the day he evicted us with nowhere to go. The pavement was the only option.

That same day my husband and his brother-in-law build a new shack. The children were very emosional, they didn't wanted to be alone. They were scared it is going to happen again. Myself were also in such a state. I couldn't sleep. My husband would come from work and take a nap because he didn't want to sleep when we were sleeping. So in the night when we sleep, he would sit up and read and watch over us and doze off every 5 minutes. He would read the newspaper or stand out to take a walk just to keep himself busy. Me and my husband talk a lot to the children because they were so scared. We had to encourage them that it would not happen again. When they feel scared, they must just go on their knees and say a prayer.

You know I learn such a lot out of this struggle. It made me strong as a mother and it made me to realise that I am not alone. Maybe something is troubling me, I can go to my neighbour and knock on the door. There's so a lot of people I can go to. The reason why I say this is that where I come from, everyone is for himself. So here, I got a whole road full of people – they're like my family. So whatever is troubling me, I can always go to anyone.

Since I got married all I wanted was a house for my family. That is my dream ever since we are 15 years on the waitinglist.

Dawn Hendricks
Gerald Hendricks
Nicole Hendricks (13 years old)
Courtney Hendricks (7 years old)
Dominique Hendricks (1 year and 3 months old)

Letter to the former Minister of Housing, Lindiwe Sisulu

To whom it may concern

Dear madam / sir.

The reason why I'm writing this letter to you is because I'm 18 years on the City's waiting list and 1 year on the subsidy. From my understanding feel I, I'm entitled to a house.

My family and I struggled for all these years and I don't feel it is right. We move from place to place rent someone elses house, stay in people's backyards and pay a lot of money for rent.

On the 19th December 2007 my family and I invade the Delft Symphony N2 Gateway houses because we are fedup of the owners moaning and groaning. As you know that we were evicted out of that house too. Now we on the Delft Symphony pavement and we like to know if you can help me and my family.

Thank you.

Yours sincerely,
Mr and Mrs Davids

187 Symphony Way, Delft, 7102

Chips, sweets, etc.

Enough is enough

Making a little statement

Our Struggle on the road for 14 years

05.12.2008

<u>To Whom it May Concern</u>:

WE THE SAMUELS Family is a very close Family and has a very strong bond and Relationship. We have a family of eight. Our first squatter camp we moved to was in 1995 a place called <u>Hyde Park</u> on Vanguard Drive. It was a place called <u>Kill Me Quick</u>, We lived there for almost seven month and my children only seen the outside of our doorstep. We didn't most have a place to stay, that is why we went to the squatter camp. It was very scary to live there, but just to be under a roof and sacrifice we stayed there. One Friday at about 6:00pm we heard people screaming and shouting, *He is Dead*. I went to look and witnessed a man was stabbed and hit with an Axe. The following day I went to my Parents in Silvertown Athlone. I explain to them what happened and they said to me we must moved in by them on the backyard. Eventually we stayed there and my wife was walking on her last days before she's going to give birth with our last son. Then she gave birth and we stayed there for three months. That was in 1997.

Then we moved to squatter camp called Heinz Park in 1997. We lived there at my sisters sons place as a backyard dweller. I bought very good material and put up a 4 room place, everything was rosy and made it convenience for my family. After six months my sister came to me and said the committee of Heinz Park came to them and said they dont want backyard dwellers, we must brake off and find a place of our own. As our hearts was sitting in our throats I smiled it off and said to her *thank you we will find a place*. My family cried and my shoulders were too small for them, but I kept me very strong for the sake of my family. I sat down with my family and discuss what are we going to do with this big shed and where we going to. Then the Saturday Morning at 6:00am I went to go knocked at my sisters sons door and said to him we going to moved but I'll will come and brake my place of as soon as I get a place. We then moved to my sister inlaw in Parkwood and explain to them our condition and they gave us a place to stay. Unfortunately they had a place in the yard and there was no place for our shack. After two weeks I went to Heinz Park again and Discover my place was thrown down and my sisters wendy house stood there and that was very heartsore to think that the amount of money we spent our shack was all gone. I immediately turn back before I entered he's place and went back to Parkwood. I explain my wife and kids and they all burst out in to Tears, and again my shoulders was not enough for them. We then lived in Parkwood for four months and my brother inlaw told us that they actually need the yard because his wife is starting their own bussiness. We then again exept it and said to them it's OK we will look out for a place.

The next day we start searching and find a place in Tafelsig also a Squatter Camp. There we moved in, in March 1998. We lived there for app: three years till 2001.

Then one day we hiked through to my Parents and got a lift with a very good friend, and he asked me if I'm still staying on Freedom Park. And I said to him yes, but why do you ask? And then he drove me and my family Striaght to a one bedroom house in the Hague in Delft. When we stopped there I asked him what's happening. He said to us get out and come have a look. Then asked us do we like the place and we said yes because the place is fully bugarlar bar, He said to us the Place is Ours. We were very happy and tears roll from our eyes to think this is our house. We had a verbal agreement about the rent for R450,00 p.m. for two years. He said, I'll sign the place over on your name after paying rent for two years. As the time goes on till in 2006 we just came from shopping and we saw a red sierra standing in front of our door. I then saw this is my friends sister and I immediately knew something was wrong. As I locked open the door she took out papers and showed us a deed of sale which put us in a hell of a shock and speechless. And she demand us to pack and leave the premmises immedi-ately. I said to her *but her brother as one of my best friends didn't mentioned anything from buying or selling this place, because we were his first option.* We asked her to get

hold of her brother so that we can sort out something, but she didn't want to understand, and was very, very rude towards me and my family. My wife and children was crying in front of her but nothing could softened her heart. People was watching in road but she could'nt care less. We were Struggling and Hassling to find a place, and eventually came out again in Tafelsig by a very good friends mother. We were in the Backyard Since 2006 till January 2007. Then she said to us with a sore heart that her Daughter is going to sell the house and where are we going to. We said to her she don't need to worry, Where There's a Will there's a Way. Then we moved to Eindhoven, Delft. I put up a very big place in the backyard and things was also rosy for three months and Suddenly the rent went up, we could'nt use the toilet anymore, we coud'nt use the water anymore and we must buy a R50,00 electricity every week. Our neighbours use to give us water. If we want to relieve our selfs we must use the drum and keep it in the house till sunset only then we can go to the bush and throw it out. We were very heartsore and frustrated but we kept it inside and we lived in Eindhoven for nine months. .

And then we heard people is moving in to N2 Gateway Houses and we decide to pack our goodies and moved. Our children were very happy and said to

19 February 2008 – hundreds of police descend on the N2 Gateway project to evict 1,000 poor backyarder families

each other we moving in to our own House, it was on 19 Dec; 2007. Our children were very happy because they were free like birds. Although there was'nt any doors and windows and we made the best of it. We live happily for two months and then chaos started.

On the 19th February 2008 at about 6:00am we heard whistles blowing and everyone was outside, we saw blue lights and lots of police vehicles coming towards our people. That made our children very sad and unhappy because they still had to Go to School. The police started loading peoples furniture and stuff and threw it on the trucks and they transported all the peoples stuff to Blackheath Warehouse and people have to pay to get their goods. We started taking out stuff and put it outside with a very sore heart. Then my children left for school with tears in there eyes, and said we love you Mom & Dad and they went off. On the other side police were shooting Rubber Bullets and Tear Gas to our Harmless people and treat us all like Animals. Eventually my children arrived, and were very happy to see us still sitting on the Sidewalk. Some police has walked through the streets and said if the people can removed there funiture they must do so because we must clear the area. Then the truck driver and those very rude men approached me and my family, and immediately my children burst in to Tears. Then the driver asked me *is there any way that I can assist you to take your stuff to a relative or friend.* I said to him he can removed my funiture and goodies to my friend. And all my other stuff you can put in Symphony Way on the Pavement, where we are now.

We staying on the Pavement for almost nine months and two weeks. We went through a very hard winter, But through the will and the Mercy of the Almighty we made it through up till now. I know all of my children and the children in Symphony Way is going through a hectic Struggle and is also affecting some of them school work, But I still believe that we are going to get a house yet, that's all that we want for our children. I would never ever want to go back to peoples back yard again where my family will be treated like animals.

This is a History in our lifetime we will never forget. And I'm thanking Mr Ashraf Cassiem and his committee for every Second and Minute they spend with the Minister of Housing e.t.c., And theres sleepless nights for thinking and fighting this Struggle.

May the Almighty must give you all the Strength, Health and Power for the years that lays ahead.

Long Live Anti Eviction Campaign.

Yours Sincerely
Mr Abdulgaliek Samuels and Family (Faiezah, Abdia, Shakeera, Ismail, and Tashreeq)

Stragel [Struggle]

FROM THE DAY I lost my mothers house, I was go from place to place, until I meet my wife. And from that time me and my family go from her mothers house and stay by friends in he's backyards. There was good time and bad time. Everytime theres a problem between my wife and that family. Their understanding was not that good. That was the time we here that there is houses and there was a girl named Des who told me that I must come and stay here in these N2 Gateway houses. We, as the Anti-Eviction, want to do something for us. Make a better life for us. We go to court. We lost the case and the eviction come, we must go out of these houses. If we will not go out, the police come with trucks and thay tru us out. There was also rubber boelits swote [shot] on us. Some of the people was swotet.

We come from there and we stays over the road neer these houses on Symphony Way. Now its the time our stragel begine. We make our own hokkies.

Here we said that we can do or we must plan for stuff that we can do. We make fire's. Here was time that we must look to ourselfs for food and wood to make fire. Hold meetings and there we said for ourselfs: *We do not take anything from the government. No food, no tents of the governments. We don't want food, we want houses from the government.* They give other people in the tents, they give them food. And now they must do everything that the government want them to do. They took all that people there in tents and put them in this Blikkiesdorp now – is a temporary location. But now we see that they put electric in this but the problem is for how long that people stay there? My point is, for how long will that place stand there? They say its a temporary location, but from what I see now, that place will stay for long as they want them there.

You see from that government members, they was here. They tell the people here, they will come back and tell us what they will do. What they decide. There was time they come here with the screening machine and they screening us on this road and they give that results to Ashraf. We can see whose the people that standing a chance for a house. Whitey Jacobs, he was also here, and he said he also will come back and work on our stuff for that houses. And they never come back. That make me feel me anger because they promise many things and they didn't come back and reply on this.

I had no job but my kids must eat and they must go to school. My wife she burn her foot with boil water. That was also winter. The winds blou and the rain is rainning but we stay where we stands. One time the wind was so tafe [strong] that we thinks that we must go but our God was with us. He provide us and he save us. From there our Birthdays we give it in the road. The lord he is the one who give me the work what I have now, the mechanical work. This is what my son said about life on the road:

> We play sports that we didn't play at other places because there was not coaches and some coaches that we know stayed far away. The communities on Symphony rd is strong and they stand together that bad things not happen to us. That we play like soccer, netball and its taking our concentrations out of the bad things. I enjoy the soccer, and soccer is my favourite sport. It give me good memories not bad memories. And everytime I play, I become better and better. And my father is the coach of the soccer team, the Symphony Way Spurs. And Aunty Rene is the coach of the netball team, Symphony United.

On the 19 February 2009 we was a year on these road. Time after that the police come and give us the forms of the court. We must go to Cape Town High Court for the replies for the evictions. We go to court and the case was set to next date of June. No we thanks the antieviction for his love that they have for us. God Bles you all.

Now we must also stand together. With one love and take more hand and

pray. So that God can help us in these case. Me and my family also pray anitime for all in the stragel. Also for Ashraf Cassiem for the love that he have for all the poor people. It is something what God give him and that he must be strong. The people can say anything about him but we will pray for him. I thank all of these committee members who help him in this time. We hope and beleave in God that we will get what we want, our houses. Becous we don't like that Blikkiesdorp what they will give us. Before the winter comes that we must have what we want. So we must stay strong and hope that God shall help us.

Thank for all who see us,

From Mr Saal and family

'Michael Jordan' protecting the hoop for the Symphony United netball team

41

The Pavement and the TRA dwellers

WE ARE NOW two families living in one shack. Actually it's my daughter living with me but she's also struggling for a house. It's interesting living here; I never lived like this before. I learned a lot of things. I learned to communicate with people. Its nice living with people you didn't know. Here we like one big happy family here on this road. If you don't have, and I got, then I give you.

I rather stay here, I won't go to the TRA's [Temporary Relocation Areas]. Here you are safe, you are free to do what you want to do. Its a little too dangerous there. I spoke to people who live there. They talk about the rape cases, the children get abused there. They can't do nothing, they can't even go to the law enforcement because the law enforcement tells them that they are not there to help people, they are there to look after the structures.

Since we moved to the pavement the bond is still the same with the people; they all united. The TRAs is not united. The half are moving that way, and the other half are moving the other way. If you go there, there's like 3 or 4 committees – you dont know who to speak to. And each committee give you a different direction. Thats why there's no control.

I even spoke to someone, one of my friends who stay there. He told me about the incident that happened there in his toilet. I asked him what happened? He told me about this guy, one of the rastas, that was playing with his penis and the kids was standing around watching. And my friend also went to look what happened there. When he came there, he found that this guy was playing with his penis. And he confronted the guy and he had a fight. It turned out so weird that it became an attempt to murder case.

Here in the road, its not like that. We in control in the road. We in control of the people. It's safe here. We got a night patrol. The people there [in the TRAs] don't sort out problems together because each person is for himself there. The committee here, if there is a problem, they sort it out immediately. We go to the people and confront the people. We speak to both sides of the people separately and then we bring them together and speak to them and then the problem ends right there.

It's not hard here on the pavement but each one deserves a house. That's the most important thing that they want. They got a right. Sometimes its hard when it rains and the wind blows and we afraid the shacks gonna blow away but thank God, it never happened. We still here.

From the pavement to a house. Not from one shack to another shack where it is very dangerous. Its not fair. I want a house and I want my kids to have houses. I dont want my kids to move to the TRAs because its dangerous there. It's interesting to live in the pavement because we never lived like this before, they like it here. But sometimes they ask when we will move into the houses. I tell them 'have patience, we going to move into the houses at the right time'.

Aunty Badru

In South Africa you have to fight for a house

I'M DOREEN SARAH Elizabeth Lewis. I'm 53 years. My grandmother was Elizabeth Sarah Marais.

Let me just think back to the days with my grandma – what struggle I was going through with her.

Me and my grandma used to stay in the backyard. We used to stay 20 years in the backyards. We stayed by different people.

My grandma used to say, *I mustn't give up to fight for a house.* She knew that she was going to die very soon. She had mos,[1] brain cancer, mos. For me it was terrifying because of looking after that old lady in other peoples backyards. Many days I was just crying, my eyes was just full of tears.

She was in her 80s. In the backyards, there was no toilet. Because the people we used to stay with, didn't allow us to use their toilets. And old people, like my grandmother, didn't want to sit on the bucket, that is why we had to ask the neighbour.

She died on the age of 85. And I continued staying in people's backyards. The people don't treat you how they should treat you because its not your place.

Because there was no such thing as happy in my life. When my grandmother died, I was hurt and lost. I knew there was no one who was going to talk to me. That was the time when I ended up getting married with my husband. My heart was empty and I just took my husband to fill that emptiness of my heart of my grandmother.

Because I was married and my marriage didn't even last. I knew that my marriage would never last, I knew that. I was just asking God to give me that strength but I knew I would not have that love and bond like with my grandma.

When I moved into the houses on the 20th of December, I was telling my husband, I'm very tired of staying in people's yard. I'm going to also take me a house. It was a joy for me, not yet knowing it was going to be a problem. I asked my husband if he's going to come stay with me and my husband said he's not mad and he's not going to stay in the houses.

As I end up here on this pavement, I'm living here with my family – my son of 21 years and my daughter of 14 years. People think that if you live in South Africa, its nice to live here. Its not nice to live here. In South Africa you have to fight for a house. Even if you die tomorrow, you have to fight for a house for your children. I'm not going to give up hope. I will fight till the end but I want a house for my family.

I learn them [my children] just as how my grandmother used to learn me the struggle.

Doreen Lewis

Note

1. 'Mos' is a slang filler word, inviting agreement from the listener, e.g. 'You understand, mos' means 'You understand, don't you?'

The world seen through a struggling soul...

It is said that the eyes is the windows to our souls,
Therefore only speak truth,
No mirror nor pretense of smiling lips,
But only the eyes.
Anonymous

IF THAT BE true, may it then be so that my expressive descriptions describes the true abstacles, pain and some memorable moments I have encountered while being on a struggling journey I've unexpectedly ventured into.

If only I had the ability to allow someone to see the world of being on this struggle through my eyes,
I am quite sure their eyes would only be filled with tears,
They would experience the unity as standing as one,
My life, My reality,
and finally know the true meaning of a person rising only to fall,
of all I have worked hard for only to be lost,
never to be found.

It would be an experience to never forget but always remember, it would be unlike any enlightment ever experienced, while walking out as proudly, bold and strong in character unimaginable...

Vividly I remember the day of our eviction like no other, the dramatical disasterous chaos, eviction, confusion, crying children, while in a remote aloof manner the Kwela-Kwela [Caspar armed vehicles] stamping off the true sense of what it possibly felt like living in an Old Apartheid South Africa era years ago.

Now months and weeks later, Living on Symphony Way road, thoughts at times still enters and flows through my mind like a rush of blood to the head, being my constant reminder of how long it has been since living in these conditions I currently find myself living in, clearly I remember how everything that once were fimiliar to me has changed within a matter of seconds, From being used to a living environment with electricity, I, myself, nowadays seek comfort in all natural resources, My Fire-wood to keep me warm at night, Candles that gives me light and at times my gas to cook a decent meal...

The day of the eviction, I admit, I had NO DIRECTION of how I, nor my family would ever survive, since everything seemed bleak, But today I stand as a person that knows where she came from and knows where I'm heading, I became a survivor, forming my nothings into somethings, with a surrounding group of people of all walks of life that (my fellow evicted united Skwatter

brothers and sisters) defined what were meant using a word like UBUNTU, I came from renting almost all my marrying years, to instantaneously being a Skwatter. NO! Never because I longed and yearned to be a struggling Skwatter or because I enjoyed living on the road because I simply can, NO! But simply because I had no other alternative since my chances in the end ended-up being 0-1…

The year 2008 has been one long transformational year, a year of hardship, constant battle and struggle, like nothing anyone in their right minds would ever sign-up for to experience on a day to day basis, But it's one of those years I will treasure with me as long as I possibly can for years to come…

Through the struggle, I've embarked on some frustrations, I've heard laughters, Experienced joyous occassions, (like a couple declaring their love for each other on the road and marrying), I've experience grief and some pain, Even dared myself to stare fear in the face,

most memorable for me would be, realizing I never in the past actively stood along with this struggle against Apartheid, but we as evicted Skwatters now actively stand as one, Having one vision and dream, only too firsly be proud house owners, that is all we ever wanted and dreamt for. Therefore I will continue my quest, seeking only a house of my own, until that momentous day finaly arrives where I can invite all and proudly say 'WELCOME TO MY HOUSE, THE PLACE I CALL HOME'

Regards
Miss L. Jansen
165 Symphony Way, Delft, 7100

Do you think that is right?

MY NAME IS Jeanette Jane Smith and I have been on the housing waiting list since 1993. I have been living on the road for a year and two months now.

When I moved here, I had nothing except for the clothes on my back. I had to look around for materials to build my shack with. At the back of my shack is nothing only bush, and I have to make a fire to cook food on and to keep warm. When it is cold there is no street lights where I live which makes me very vulnerable to gangsters and thief's. But its usually safe here on the pavement.

I want to tell you something about two of my friends who were wrongly blamed for things they didn't do. Two of my friends went to jail because *we* were breaking shacks of people who were betraying the people in Symphony Way. Riedewaan and Jerome was not part of it. When all the people come from a meeting, Riedewaan and me were talking on the pavement. Riedewaan get a call from his wife and he jumped over the fence to go and see what his wife wanted [in another side of Delft]. I went to the sacks but when I get there it was already gone. Thats why I am saying they are innocent.

The people take off that shack of Brother John. When Brother John came back, he and his sons, they did shoot at us. But we haven't got no guns. The one that

got hurt was Brother Ryan. They shoot him in the leg. The time when they shoot, I ran around the shack and afterwards I just ran home. It was dark and we did not know for whom they were shooting.

But afterwards, Bother John went to the police station to report that we had broken the law. Because brother Ryan didn't want to make a case, the police automatically came for Riedwaan and Jerome. Thats why they went to jail. They sit in jail for nothing – for the things that we did.

For innocent people to go to jail for what other people did, its not nice. Do you think that is right?

God Bless

Jeanette J. Smith

The Symphony Way dryer

Struggle for Freedom
Struggle for a Home

IF I THOUGHT that struggle seems to be a easy thing then I was wrong. Any struggle of some sort is not easy especially if its for a house that u struggle for.

The time that I invaded that houses in Dec 2007 I thought that the house is mine & I didn't think that I did anything wrong. We were invaders that did not think of the consequences. All that we saw was a opportunity to own a house. To have a house where we could put ownership to it and to get away from back-yards, rent thats to high.

My bubble was soon to be burst when the Law Enforcement came and evict us from the houses and there afterwards we had to attend court in order for us to fight for our right to stay in that houses. All that came to an end when the court ordered the eviction and we were evicted in Feb 2008. That was a sad day for everyone that stayed in that houses. Most of us had no place to go; the houses, separate entrances, Wendy houses in backyards or just a rented room wasn't

available anymore. Many of us had lost our jobs because we had to guard the place that we called our house. Sometimes, if you are not there at the house, someone else come and take out your stuff and your furniture and move into your place.

Now we are here on the pavement on Symphony Way since we were evicted. To be here its more difficult then it was in the illegal houses. It frustrate you to think that you cannot get what you need the most while some who do not deserve it get it so easily. Meaning – all the corruption thats going on since the project N2 gateway started, people who needs houses do not stand a chance even if they did fill in a subsidy and people who do own previous houses buy their way in in order to get another house. Those who are in charge makes money by selling or charging a fee for the house and the poor is left out in receiving a home for them but most important for their children. We cannot move forward in anything. Its almost like we took a step back in life just being there on the pavement. Everything stands still for you. Things may seem normal or go on as normal but its not. I think its like the old age time, where everything is primitive in 2000 B.C. (Before Christ).

But we do the best we can. We are a close community. The understanding is there and so is the love for one another. We are doing everything we can to get what we are struggling for – a house. We are doing everything in our power to give our children the most important gift – a safe home – a place of peace and love. In this struggle we have learned to deal with many other issues like drug issues, domestic violence and teenage pregnancies. That is also another struggle on its own. We are all there to help each other in every way or to support in anyway, but most important is to not stay on the pavement forever, to fight for what is our right!

End our wait We are waiting too long.
Please!!! Mr Whitey Jacobs Please help us!

Only you can stop us from suffering
We give you the opportunity to make a change.
Please help us.

If you want to make a difference please think of the poor people first
Think of those who needs your help. Please Mr Whitey Jacobs. Please help us.

All we are asking is a house nothing more.
Please please help us!!!

Turn your ear to the poor hear them cry.
Turn your eyes to the children see them suffer.
Turn your focus on the new born babies & give them what they need a house.
Please please help us.

Too long we are waiting, too long we are suffering
End this waiting, end this suffering, end this longing & loneliness.
We are longing, we are alone.
To end all this all we need is a home.
Please Mr Whitey Jacobs. Please please help us.

If people now currently staying on the pavement should have a choice in the matter to go to their old places, Tsunami, Blikkies, or the pavement, I think they would have choose over and over – the pavement. Because here in Symphony Way we have the opportunity to fight for our right for the first time. That we have learned how to stand together and work together as a team, and that we have rights especially the right to have a home. We have a mandate – we are not moving from one structure to another – We Want Houses.

I believe that we will receive houses because of the faith that I have in God.

My encouragement to anyone who is in a struggle is to continue in doing what is right and continue to fight for your right. If you fight for what you believe in and start doing right to others, that way we can change the communities and when communities are changed the world start to change.

The people on Symphony Way's need is too big just to ignore it. We all want the road open. While we are on this road it will stay close until we receive houses.

Aluta Continua

Jacolene Faroa
The Office
Symphony Way
Delft
7100

TO THE READER:

Thank you for taking a few min to read this letter. Just by reading it, it mean a lot to those who are struggling on the pavement in Symphony Way, Delft – Cape Town.

God Bless!!!

Jacqui

Homework by lamplight

Symphony Way children speaking at a night-time mass community meeting

A friendship built on the road

A 'temporary' school in Delft next to Blikkiesdorp Temporary Relocation Area.
The school is attended by many of our Symphony Way children

A South African senior citizen

03-11-08

I, MATILDA GROEPE would hereby express, as a South African Senior Citizen still fighting for my 1st house, my gruesome experience – relating the eviction of Symphony Way on 19th Feb 2008.

I personally have been on the waiting list for +/- 13 years of which I've been robbed. In 2006, when I went to investigate my waiting period, I had to re-apply because I was informed that the waiting list was something of the past. Searching for a solution I started attending the DA [Democratic Alliance] meetings. On the 18th of Dec 2007 the ward councillor Mr Frank Martin instructed us to occupy the houses vowing to take full political responsibility. As we were later evicted on the 24th of December with a false eviction order, that was originally issued for a separate eviction in 2006. As it was an illegal eviction, we were able to stay occupying the houses. We re-appeared in the Cape High Court. Applying for an appeal on the 17th Feb, we were suppose to move out of the N2 Gateway which we supposedly invaded illegally. Whereby Mr Frank Martin denied us saying he never gave us permission to occupy the housees. I found him very decieteful because he never delivered what he promised. That is the reason, why we landed on the pavement of Symphony Way. I am holding him responsible for my inconvenient life on the pavement.

On the 19th of Feb, when the appeal failed the whole squad of law-en-forcement, police, securities lured [lept] on us like sharks it was undignified, unprofessional, heartbroken they fired us with rubber bullets they treated us worse than dogs. Trucks came to load our personal posessions. I practically lost everything including shoes, clothes, curtains, pots, my vinyl, my gas cilinder, my bedding, my bed and my lounge suit. We were told by the sherrif it was going to be kept in Blackheath, but when we went back for our stuff, there was nothing. A reporter that followed the trucks told us our stuff was dumped and other people came to collect it.

The Anti-Eviction Campaign came to our rescue. Ashraf Cassiem stood in for us as a delegate when meeting with the provincial & local government. The papers say that the Anti-Eviction, especially Ashraf Cassiem is ruling us with an iron fist which is not true because we give him the mandate and he must go and negotiate with the provincial & local government. I salute the Anti-Eviction Campaign because there is no hidden agendas. After each negotiation or meet-ing with the MEC [member of the Executive Committee] of Housing, we do get feedbacks. We ain't left in the dark. We know where we stand with the Anti-Eviction unlike Frank Martin and the DA [Democratic Alliance]. Ashraf Cassiem and the committee of Anti-Eviction did a splendid job.

We have decided to occupy Symphony Way as we had no other option. We had to collect cardboard, plastic sticks, anything that could be used to build a shack. It was way beyond our expectations especially when we saw youngsters at the age of 18 years old are rightfull owners to houses. Experiencing the winter weather on Symphony Way were humaliating it was very frustrating having a leaking shack we were all very emotional. My roof blew off twice but I had to stay in my wet shack because it was raining with a gale force wind. But thank God for somebody like Ashraf Cassiem whose heart went out for us and saw the need of helping us in our plight. The judge of the Cape High Court even made us believe that we'll get the housees, by telling us we must go home and make gardens. That is why we were so devastated when we were evicted.

Aluta Continua

God Bless you in Abundance Ashraf Cassiem

Matilda Groepe

*Photograph
of WC-AEC
coordinator
Ashraf Cassiem
by 6-year-old
Lolos Engelbrecht*

Lolos

The following are a letter of support and poetry that Vicky, one of the evicted residents in Delft, wrote and distributed to her community in the winter of 2008.

To all my fellow comrades in da struggle: Don't Give Up!!

YOU MAY BE tired…

You may feel like you've been in the storm 2 long…

Don't Give Up.

You may feel like the enemy is beating u down…

Don't Give Up.

You may feel like no one cares and no one sees you…

Don't Give Up.

You may feel smothered with responsibility work & bills…

Don't Give Up.

You may feel defeated, angry, hurt, put down and fed up…

Don't Give Up, God is with you!

In Gods time you breakthrough will come because of your perseverance, faith and your willingness to learn.

Stay open and optimistic, because your next blessing will probably come from the most unexpected person or place.

REMEMBER ALWAYS stay in the Light,

Keep on, keep on.

Be Blessed!

Aluta…Continua

From Comr. Vicky

A Poem for Each and Every Day

May u have:	Reminds me of
Enough happiness to keep u sweet	*19 December 2007 we occupied N2 Gateway houses 'illegal', were very happy to have my own house. My two kids had their own room. Everything was so sweet.*
Enough friends to give u comfort	*Made friends with neighbours. Felt comfortable cause we were not alone in this struggle*
Enough success to keep u eager	*We knew that the city would wanna Evict us, cause of our successful action on the 19th we became eager to fight the City of Cape Town*
Enough trials to keep u strong	*City applied for eviction order and ±1500 families marched together to court very strongly. The city won the case and evictions started 19 Feb. 08. But that made us even stronger.*
Enough sorrow to keep u human	*We were sad to be evicted, cause our children's dreams were shattered.*
Enough failure to keep u humble	*When we move to the pavement in Symphony Way we felt that we've failed. We became humble towards each other – Helped wherever we could.*
Enough faith to banish depression	*But out Faith banished our depression. We believed that we gonna get our houses (homes) back – And we still BELIEVE. Cause our Almighty is always with us especially in our STRONG PRAYERS. With every single meeting our chairperson of the Anti Eviction Campaign Mr. Ashraf Cassiem taught us to hold hands and pray at every start and end of a meeting. Please Add Living on Symphony Way e.g.: The fires, sandstorms, rains, deaths, marriages, illnesses. But yet we're strong.*

Enough determination to make each day better than yesterday
Viva anti-eviction campaign, viva
Long live the spirit of Comrade Ashraf Cassiem
Long live!!!
written by: _Vicky Anderson_

Play on the pavement

Hier het ek geleer om te deel

FRANK MARTIN BY die council het vir my die reg gegee om 'n huis te kom beset in Delft. Volgens hom sou ons die volgende oggend by mekaar kom, die grootmense (ouer lede van die gemeenskap, ek is nou 58 jaar oud) kon kies tussen huise met groter badkamers, toilette wat werk, huise wat voledig gebou was. Frank Martin het vir ons ingelig dat die polisie ons nie kon uitsit nie want HY het ons die reg gegee om daar te woon.

Na ons daar ingetrek het, het die polisie ons uitgesit en ons gestuur na Symphony Way.

Dit was 6:30 die oggend, ek het by die venster uit geloer want ek het buite remoer gehoor. Mense van die media en die koerant het aangedui dat ek moes uit kom, die polisie was oppad om ons te kom uit sit. Die gedagte wat my onmiddellik getref het was: "kry jou besittings bymekaar !" . Ek het toe begin oppak, alles wat ek in die hande kon kry, en my vriendin, wat in Leiden se ou huise woon, gevra om my te help. Sy het my besittings in haar huis gestoor sodat die polisie dit nie kon vat en weggdra nie. Die polisie het die bisittings na Happy Valley to geneem, hulle het gesê hulle gaan dit stoor. Omdat ons nie 'n stoor plek het nie. Maar niemand het hulle goed gekry nie.

Na die polisie hier weg is, is ons agter gelaat met 'n paar komberse en 'n klein sakkie klere. So het my lewe op Symphony Way begin. Die eerste en tweede weke van my NUWE LEWE was daar geen bou materiaal om te probeer om skuiling opterig nie. Cardbaord, hardboard, plastiek sakke was vasgedraai met lappies as beskerming teen slange, skerpione en die onvoorspelbare weer: reen, wind met al die Cape Flats se sand duine.

Dis nou al 'n jaar. My hokkie was klein maar die hele Symphony Way gemeenskap het gehelp om my (as 'n enkel ouer van 'n dogter en haar klein baba), ons in 'n grooter skuiling te plaas. Dit is die gesindheind van hierdie Symphony Way mense. Hier het ek geleer om te deel: ek werk nie, maar as ek 'n stukkie droe brood het kyk ek eers om my rond of my buurman/vrou iets het om te eet, voor ek eet. Dit voel soos 'n GROOT FAMILIE.

Ek voel dankbaar vir die Here dat Hy ons beskerm hier. Ons almal is nog saam, deur die Here se genade, ons sis nog sterk in die struggle van behuising.

Florrie Langenhoven

Here I've learned to share

FRANK MARTIN BY the council gave me the right to invade a house in Delft. According to him they would have met the next morning to decide that the big people (the oldest in the community, as I am now 58 years old), we could choose the houses that got bigger bedrooms, toilets that work, or houses that are finished or built completely. Frank Martin told us that the policemen could not evict us because he gave us the right to live there.

After we moved in, the policemen evicted us and sent us to Symphony Way.

It was 6:30 in the morning when I peeped through the window because I heard a noise outside. People from the media and the newspapers told me that I should come out, the policemen were on the way to come and evict us. The thought that striked me immediately was: 'get all your my belongings together'. I started to packing everything that I could get, and my friend that stays in the old Leiden houses, I asked her to help me. She kept all my belongings in her house so that the policemen could not carry it away. The police take your belongings to Happy Valley, they told us they put it there when we do not have place for our stuff. But the people haven't got their stuff back.

After the policemen were gone, we all stayed behind with our blankets and a small bag of clothes. Thats how my life started on Symphony Way. The first and the second week of my NEW LIFE there was no building material to try to build a shelter. Cardboards, hardboards, plastic bags were tied with pieces of cloth as a protection against snakes, scorpions, and the unexpected weather: rain, wind with all the Cape Flats sand dunes.

Its now already a year. My hokkie [shack] was small but the whole Symphony Way community helped me (as a single parent with a daughter thats got a small baby), we was placed in a bigger shelter. That is the humanity of this Symphony Way people. Here I've learned to share: I don't work, but if I've got dry bread I first look around if my neighbours have got something to eat before I can eat. It feels like a BIG FAMILY.

I am grateful that God is protecting us here. We are all still together here through the mercy of God and we are still going strong in the struggle of houses.

Florrie Langenhoven

My Struggle

OP DIE 19 Desember 2007 het 'n vergadering in die Delft Civic met Frank Martin gehad. Hy het ons aangemoedig om die huise se deure oop te trap by N2 Gateway. Ek het toe so gemaak, ek was toe alleen. By elke huis wat ek toe skoon gemaak het in die N2 Gateway dan het die mense gekom en gesê dat dit hulle huis is, dan is ek weer uit. Hoe kan ek die kinders gaan haal as ek nog nie 'n huis het nie? Ek het nagte alleen gesoek vir my vir 'n huis, want ek moet my kinders gaan haal wat by familie gebly het.

Sommige nagte het ek by die lëe huise se vensters gestaan en kyk of daar nie gevaar is nie, want daar is niks by die deure en vensters nie. Ek het in nege huise al gebly, toe kry ek my tiende huis. Die sondag aand toe trek ek in die huis. Toe hoor ek die huis is afgegee want die vrou wat daarin gebly het se broer is afgesterwe. Toe trek ek en my twee kinders in met toestemming van die mense se committee. Die maandag toe het my kinders niks om te eet nie en ek en hulle

gaan om kos te gaan soek in Uitsig (Ravensmead) Toe ek terug kom toe bly daar iemand anders in my huis. Ons het toe na die committee toe gegaan, en hulle het toe besluit dat ek en my twee kinders in die huis bly. Die rede vir die committee se official besluit om vir my in die huis te sit is omdat die gesin nooit ingetrek het nie, Sondagaand was hulle deadline. Ons het lekker gebly in die huis. Daar was geen krag en ons moet kerse en gas gebruik en vuur. Ek het nog nie gas gehad nie, toe moes ek op 'n vuur kos gemaak het en water gekook het. Toe het ek selfs my werk verloor, maar my God het my deur gedra. Nagte het ek wakker gelê, want ek moet sorg dat my kinders veilig is. Maar ek kan net die Here dank dat Hy ons sover bevaar het. Die huis was so eie aan my dat bid-ure en kerkdienste gereeld by Tien Gebooie (naam van my huis) plaasgevind het. Ek het gedog dis MY HUIS en ek sal NOOIT daar uittrek nie.

Toe kom die skok van my lewe mos…

Op die 19 Februarie 2008 was ons ge-evict van die huise. Die polisie het vir my gese dat die huise is te mooi vir ons kleurlinge, vir wat wil ons die huise he? Hy se vir ons, ons is onnodig om die huise te beset. Ek het ALLES verloor wat ek besit het, onder andere kaste, beddens, kombuiskaste, potte, borde, koppies, lepels, vurke, my baba se stootwaentjie, TV, DVD ens. Die getal polisie en media was oorweldiglik baie, rubber bullets was gevuur. Baie mense was beseer en het mediese hulp nodig gehad. Die koste van die polisie en kos wat beskikbaar gemaak was vir hulle kon meer huise gebou het.

Ek het toe na die pad gekom en alreeds besluit om my kinders weggestuur omdat daar geen skuiling was vir hulle nie. Die eerste drie aande het ek onder die maan en sterre geslaap, dit is 'n groot ervaring want nog nooit in my lewe het ek ooit so iets beleef nie. Na die drie aande toe slaap ek onder twee swart vuilis blikke, matras en 'n seil.

Daarna het ek gebly in 'n baie klien hokkie waar jy jou self nie kon in beweeg nie. Toe gaan haal ek weer die kinders. Ek was moeilik, maar vir die kinders se onthaal moes ek maar sterk wees. Daar was baie aande wat ek so voor die Here geween het. Eendag het ek uitgegaan, toe ek terug kom was my plek onverwags groter gemaak deur drie manne wat saam met my in die struggle is. Ek was eers baie opgemaak, want nou kan ek beweeg soos ek wil in 'n groter vetrrek. Toe begin die dinge afdrant gaan. As dit reen was ek en die kinders, bed, komberse met plek en al waternat. Dan vra ek nog vir die Here of dit nodig is, dit was baie koud en dan moet jy nog onder nat komberse gaan slaap. Die kinders was siek, ek moes medisyne koop met net my inkomste (child-grant) . Dit was onbeskryf-lik moeilik, niemand sal verstaan as hulle dit nie eerste-hands ondervind nie.

Die Here het dit moontlik gemaak dat ek vir my 'n siel kan koop en iemand met 'n baie goeie hart het vir my daai seil op die dak gesit, en nou as dit reën kan ek lekker gaan slaap. Maar nou moet ons aan die ander ook dink wat se plekke

Councillor Frank Martin's letter to Auntie Cynthie giving her authorisation to occupy a home in the N2 Gateway. Martin issued over 300 of these letters, resulting in the largest home occupation in South Africa's history. The 1,000 desperately poor families who occupied the homes bore the brunt of the state's backlash while Cllr Martin got off scot-free

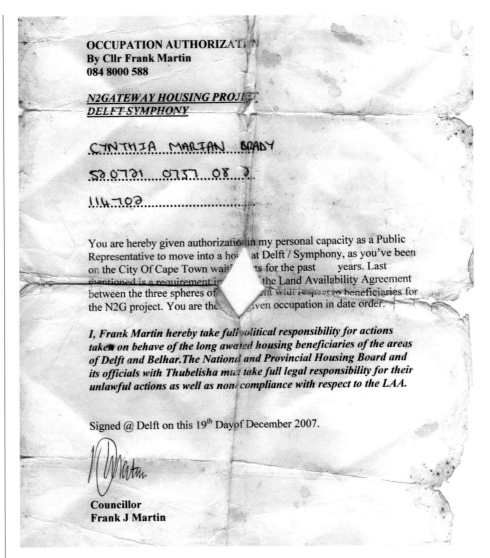

OCCUPATION AUTHORIZATION
By Cllr Frank Martin
084 8000 588

N2GATEWAY HOUSING PROJECT
DELFT SYMPHONY

CYNTHIA MARIAN BRADY

58 0721 0757 08 2

116 702

You are hereby given authorization in my personal capacity as a Public Representative to move into a home at Delft / Symphony, as you've been on the City Of Cape Town waiting lists for the past   years. Last mentioned is a requirement in the Land Availability Agreement between the three spheres of government with respect to beneficiaries for the N2G project. You are therefore given occupation in date order.

I, Frank Martin hereby take full political responsibility for actions taken on behave of the long awaited housing beneficiaries of the areas of Delft and Belhar. The National and Provincial Housing Board and its officials with Thubelisha must take full legal responsibility for their unlawful actions as well as non compliance with respect to the LAA.

Signed @ Delft on this 19th Day of December 2007.

Councillor
Frank J Martin

ook nog lek. Dit is niks lekker om in so omstandighede te lewe nie veral as jy kinders het nie.

Ek het nou ingestem om te help met die kleuterskool. Die kleuterskool is ingestel vir Symphony Way se gesinne met kinders, ouers wat bedags werk en niemand het om na hulle kinders te kyk nie. Dit is nou 'n nuwe ervaring, maar dit is 'n plesier om met die kinders te werk. Ons leer die kinders om te skryf, om te sing, gediggies opse, leer hulle uit die Bybel, teken, en enige vorm van kindwees. Hulle is pragtig, veral as hulle moet bid voor hulle gaan eet.

Vandag sit ek nog steeds op Symphony Way, wag op 'n huis van eie. Ek vertrou nog steeds die Here. EK GAAN MY HUIS KRY !

Sharon Coleridge en familie

My Struggle

ON THE 19TH of December 2007, we had a meeting in Delft Civic with Frank Martin. He encouraged us to pull of the doors off the houses in the N2 Gateway. I did do so because I was alone. By every house [that I occupied] in the N2 Gateway, when I was busy cleaning, everytime there is people coming to the house and said it is their house, and then I have to move out again. Every night, I looking for a house because each house occupied by someone else. How can I fetch my children if I dont have a house yet? When I found a house eventually, I go to fetch my children who was by [were with my extended] family at that time.

Sometimes I look out through the empty house windows, [wondering] if there is not any danger outside because there was no windows and doors. I stayed in 9 houses already and then I found my 10th house. The Sunday evening I was move into the last house, then I heard the house was given back to the committee because the brother of the women who was stay in the house passed away [and the occupying woman left the house]. Then me and my two children moved into the house with the permission of the people's committee. The Monday, me and my children got nothing to eat so we decided to go looking for food in Uitsig (Ravensmead). When I was coming back, there was someone else staying in my house. Then we go to the committee and they decided that I and my children must stay in that house. The reason for the committee's official decision for putting me in the house is because the women who was staying in the house before me was supposed to come back before the Sunday evening but she didn't and that's why the committee decided to put me in the house. We stayed very lekker [nicely] in the house. There was no power so we have to use candles and gas and wood fire. I did not have gas so I was cooking food and water on the fire. I even lose my job but God did carry me through. Nights I lay awake because I have to secure my children's safety. But I can only thanks God that he look after us so far. The house was so owned by me that we even do church prayers regularly by the 10 Commandments (the name of my house) where it happened regularly. I thought that I would NEVER move out of MY HOUSE.

Then the shock of my life was coming...

On the 19th of February 2008, we were evicted from the house. The police did said to me that the houses is too beautiful for our Coloured people, *why do we want these houses?* He said to me that we are unnecessary to occupy these houses. I just lose everything that was owned by me, my beds, kitchen cupboards, pots, plates, cups, spoons, forks, my baby's pram, TV, DVD, etc. In total, the police and media was a lot because of there was rubber bullets fired. Lots of people was hurt and needed medical help. Due to the eviction, the money, what was put in to bring all the police around and food for them, could be used to build houses for the people.

Then we was coming to the road and already decided to send my children away because there was no shelter for them. The first three nights I was sleeping under the moon and stars. It was a very big experience because I didn't go through something like that before. The first three nights, I was sleeping under durt-bins, a mattress and a sail [a plastic covering].

After that, I was staying in a small shelter where I can't even move myself. Then I go to fetch my children again. I was so exhausted but for the sake of my children I have to be strong. There was many nights when I was crying before God. One day, I went out for the day, when I was coming back all of a sudden my place was built bigger by 3 men who was with me in the struggle. I was very surprised because now I can move in my shelter like I want.

Then things started going downwards because of the rain it makes the whole place soaking wet, like the curtains, the bedding, and the whole shelter was filled with water. Then I was asking for God if that is really necessary because it was very cold and then I have to sleep under wet bedding when I go to sleep. My children was very sick and I have to buy medicine from the only income I have (my child-grant). It was not making sense for some other people who don't understand for the first-hand what we going through in this situation.

God make it possible for me that I can buy for me a sail and someone with a good heart put the sail for me as roof cover and now when it start raining I can go sleep lekker. But now we have to think about some other people's whose places are also leaking. It is not lekker to stay in conditions like that especially when you have children.

I also decided now to help with the crèche. The crèche is only for Symphony Way families and children, parents who are working during the day and don't have someone looking after their children. It is a new experience and also a pleasure to work with children. We also teach the children to write and to sing and how to say poetry and reading out of the Bible, and sketches, and any form of childhood. They are very beautiful especially when they pray before they eat.

Today I'm still sitting on Symphony Way, waiting on a house of my own. I still trust in God. I AM GOING TO GET MY HOUSE!

Sharon Coleridge and family

The struggle

I (ALFRED ARNOLDS) would like everyone around the globe to read my story here on the sidewalk in Symphony Way, Delft, Cape Town, Western Cape, South Africa. I personally had a lot to tell millions of people around the world, about my life and personal experiences here on the sidewalk. From the beginning which was from the 19th February 2008 on a Tuesday, that we became evicted, everyone had just ran here to Symphony Way with whatever they had, just to be at the safe side away from the Government Officials (Police, Law Enforcement, Metro Police) after being threatened by them the whole day. I testify about my own personal experience that I am remembering like it had happen just yesterday, and it is now already 12 months back.

During the time we were on the sidewalk, a lot of things had happened. Firstly to mention is the births of babies that was born here, children became ill, they became the young victims of a real corrupt Government. Adults pick up asthma

& T.B. (tuberculosis). The children were also exposed to a lot of dangers here on Symphony Way. It is also the children's daily tasks to go and collect some firewood in the bush right at the back of their shacks (the bush of evil). So many of our children, witness the unhuman treatment of some of their families, from Government Officials. Sometimes its their own parents that becomes treated that way by Government Officials. Many times that it had happened that people here at Symphony Way became victimised, and discriminated by these Officials.

I, personally, had a lot to testify about my own experience with these people (the Government Officials) while I'm staying here. Whenever you talk to them or approach them in quite a polite way, they always have something bad to say. At many occasions I was humiliated in front of all our children, discriminated, victimised just because I can stand for my rights. Government officials telling you, *you don't know your rights. You people, you are uneducated, you are nothing, you are poor, homeless.*

On Saturday evening 28th of June, 2008 past 10, a lady with the name Mathilda Groepe, better known as Auntie Tilla and a guy called Ettiene tried to prevent some police officials who were under the influence of liquor while they were on duty, to pass through the barricades. That guys left. When they came back, they were more than 4 police vehicles including the station commander and they ask for Auntie Tilla and Ettiene who had accused them of being under the influence.

I tried to avoid Auntie Tilla and Ettiene's arrest on that evening. The police officials, before I was arrested and pepper sprayed, they fight with me, they physically hit me, they choked me, in front of all the residents here. After that they took me, forced me into the police van. They just throw me in. After, I collapsed and passed out in the police van. I woke up on the lawn of the police station. They had just thrown me out of the van until I woke up again.

Struggle philosophy

People usually see us, the poor people, as people who knows nothing. Most of the time, they usually call us useless, just because we are poor. That is actually our situation, we are already poor and they think we know nothing.

The poor people, they are always afraid of action, doing something for themselves. Thats why they feel like being the quiet type, that type of people. Always waiting before they start something. Recently now, the poor people, we are stuck in poverty. When we talk about poverty of the people, then, that specific people, we have a vision of having nothing, being nothing, knowing nothing, being known by no one.

There are a lot of things we know about that we don't talk about. There are always people that know something, but we are afraid of letting people know

what we know. But, if you come up with something, other people who dont know us, they become shocked. It is unexpected.

We look like we do not know something. But we know something. If I can specify something, things that happened in the past here in our country – our apartheid years. Some of our parents, they have passed away already, and told us before about what have happened in this country in those years, in their time. They explained to us how the government of that time treated them. Now we know at least that we can also tell people who did not go through these things, what we already experience with the new government.

It is important for those people that do not know our situation. That they can read what we are going through. We as the poor people have been marginalised for quite a long time. You find that, apartheid is not completely gone.

Then it comes to the point where you feel you have waited too long by being silenced and not saying what you know. Because there's so many people out there who would be interested in those experiences that you had, to hear what you had gone through and hear what you know.

Watching a play on the pavement. The Symphony Way children generated their own stories, which they performed for the other residents of the road

We want secure housing for our children. We looking at second and third generation of families. Whatever we do today will be a statement for the second or third generation children. So now, as we know, all of us, we are about to extend our families. By doing so, with our experiences, we can convey the message to the generations to come. We need to teach them at home as well and tell them everything we know about our past.

There will always be people that is homeless, there will always be people that is struggling. Therefore, we must teach our children that the struggle continues.

My encouragement to my fellow comrades

Through this struggle on the road, it made me even a better person, to set an example of standing by my people no matter being victimised, discriminated and illtreated. I don't feel like I am someone who is in a poverty state. Because I am proud of who I am, what I am doing, and where I am. Because I still got a family that I have to provide for everyday. I can still make decisions and I know whenever I make a decision, I can also face the consequences of my own decisions. I am free, but not as free as someone who can do anything they want in life. Because there are still things the government is doing to our people which me personally cannot change for them and for myself.

I write this story especially for my fellow comrades, that were still in the struggle with me, now after I was allocated to be the rightful owner of a new house, after almost ten (10 years) on the waiting list for a house. My story is about my encouragement which I convey to all my fellow comrades at Symphony Way.

What I would like to encourage them with, is not to give up hope of believing they will get houses as I have received one from government. And my message to them is to keep standing together as they have started it, so it must be, until they all receive their houses.

No matter whether I am in a house, I still know their situation. I am also grieving about their situation as they do. And keep on praying for them while I am already living in a house with my family.

The day when they become allocated, I want them all to gather, everyone that they have stayed at Symphony Way, and have a moment of silence just to be thankful for being together. Because, I do believe, with all my heart, that they will stay together. They must never forget what they have gone through. And keep on showing that love that they have had on Symphony Way, when they are all in their houses together.

'Aluta Continua'

Alfred Arnolds

What is rightfully ours is houses

MY NAME IS Bahiya Claasen, I am 45 years old.

I was board, bred and raised in Wetton [suburb of Cape Town]. But never in my wildest dreams did I ever thought that I will stay in a plastic shack at this age.

I was one of the people who was evacuated from the N2 Gateway Houses in Delft. When we moved into our shacks on Symphony, we were identified as urgent but the fact remains that had we not occupied, Thubelisha [Homes] and the government would not have identified us as urgent.

Building houses is not just about bricks, mortar, spreadsheets and so on, it is about fulfilling our needs as living breathing people and what is rightfully ours is houses. I have experience a lot on Symphony, we had a long and terrible winter but my plastic shack is still standing. Living in a shack and in a community like Symphony is the best thing that could have ever happen to me.

All thanks to Ashraf Cassiem, Aunty Jane & the whole community of Symphony-Delft!!

Bahiya Claasen

The following is a letter that Bahiya wrote to Richard Dyantyi, former MEC [member of the Executive Council] for Housing in the Western Cape

To the Minister of Housing…

Mr Dyantyi, my name is Bahiya Claasen. I am one of the evicted people of Delft Symphony, it took a long time and a lot of courage for me to right this letter to you. I am staying on the pavement and I thought to myself why must I be ashame of who I am and who I am related to and I've been in this struggle sins last year. Sir! My brother is working in one of your offices, he is a very respectable wel loved and a very honest person. I don't need to tell you because you know him so well! His name is Michael Bell.

I'm writing this letter on behalf of everyone who are staying on the pavement. Sir, we are so sick and tired of everybody who hords power in their hands, people who have deprived us of our rights. People who think they can throw us around and just walk over us. Mainly the people who sits on their high pedestals that thinks nother [nothing] of our poor children, and they are the ones who suffer the most. Then I think to myself is this our New Generation? Or our Forgotten Generation?

At night while your children enjoy a nice healthy meal, our children must eat sand in their food. While your children enjoy a nice hot bath we must wait for our water to boil on a fire. What I admire the most of our children is that they never complain. Our children think that life must be like this, And I think how wrong of you and everybody in Government to do this to our children. I'm writing this letter with tears in my eyes and a broken heart thinking what is going to happen to our NEW GENERATION Generation? Or should I say our FORGOTTON GENERATION?

If Sir! You do not want to think of us! Then please please think of our children!!!

Sir! My most concern is that winter is on its way. And like a lot of us, I am on the housing waiting list for more than 13 years…

Yours Sincerely,

Bahiya Claasen

A Gift From God

MANY WOMEN IN the struggle fell pregnant at the time of the eviction. Some was already pregnant. It was very difficult for mothers to attend clinics as the clinics wanted adresses.

When they tell nursing staff at the clinics that they staying on the road they became a topic. Some of our women was embarresed and felt offended. Amanda Engelbrecht a 30 year old woman had difficulties in her pregnancy as she was a cardiac patient. When it was time for labour, Amanda's cardiac problem started again. She gave birth to a boy, Keagan Engelbrecht. Due to the fact that she stayed on the this road, Keagan developed Pneumonia at some time.

Lee-ann was another case. Thank you to our creator that she didn't have any complications. *Hope* was born on 10 September 2008 and her parents said that she was their hope for a home for their own. Aneesa was also another case of a child being born on Symphony Way. Shanoer was born on 19th of August, 2008.

Other woman that are still pregnant has complications but that didn't made them moved away. It is very difficult to raise a baby in these conditions. We have a lot of toddlers on the pavement. They are healthy except for having a home.

Nadine Wilson, born with Down's Syndrome on 24 October 2008 on Symphony Way

Simony was pregnant and in these difficulties she lost her baby and she had an operation. It wasn't easy but these are things women has to cope with.

Our newest resident Nadine Wilson was born on 24 October 2008. She was born with severe illnesses but this didn't kept her mom from staying on the road. Nadine is born with Down Syndrome and cardiac complications. She needs to be on digoxin and other meds for her operation to repair her little heart. The community are praying for Nadine and that is a list of our babies of Symphony way.

Five people have received keys to their homes and they decided to move when the community moves. Thanks to those families who thinks of our children and especially Nadine a gift from God.

Our children are our future.

René Onverwag
The Onverwag Family
S130
Symphony Way

Aluta Continua!

WE WERE 1 of the families who unlawfully occupied the houses in Dec 2007. On the 19th Feb 2008 we were evicted from those houses through a court-eviction notice. It was a very sad day especially for our kids. We then decided to move to the pavement Symphony Way together with the AEC [Anti-Eviction Campaign] as our leaders.

The 1st night on the pavement we slept on a mattress under the stars. We then made a comitment we stand where we sleep and 9 months later I am still sticking to my comitment. A lot of people has moved to Blikkiesdorp. Blikkiesdorp is a place called Temporary Relocation Area down the road. Me and my family together with another 138 families are staying on Symphony Way pavement struggling for houses and shall not be removed until we get our houses. I know

for a fact that if Ashraf and aunty Jane from the AEC wasn't here to guide us we would have been long gone.

In a community meeting I was elected to join the Delft AEC. I accepted and today I am not sorry for accepting. I have since learn a lot from Ashraf and aunty Jane. Before I joined the committee I never even use to pick up my hand in a meeting but now I am able to help and give people advise and everyday I am learning a lot still. I never in my wildest dreams would have thought that I would be meeting people like the MEC [member of the the Executive Council] Whitey Jacobs as well as the premier and even Jacob Zuma.

Christmas and New Year is coming soon. On Symphony we decided to celebrate those days as if we are in our homes. Because Symphony has become our homes for the last 9 months. We have become 1 big family. I do not say that we don't have any differences, we do but we always solve our difference without getting rude or using violence.

To my fellow comrades ALUTA CONTINUA! Our struggle continues and do not give up hope and do not lose faith. We are going to get houses. We survived this winter and that just shows us that God is watching over us. To Ashraf & aunty Jane Thank You for everything. Without you we would have not made it this far. Please do not give up on us I know sometime we can be difficult but we do need you.

Amandla!

Kareemah Linneveldt
(Kareemah, Zainodien, Madenieyah, Zaid, and Mushfeekah Linneveldt and Shanur Davids)

Struggle for Houses

IT ALL STARTED on a Wednesday the 19th of December 2007. We went to a meeting in the Delft Civic Centre. It was a meeting about houses. Frank Martin the D.A. [Democratic Alliance] Leader was having a meeting and told the people that if we want houses we should go take for our houses. We all ran out of there to go and take us houses. We took us houses that was not even fully completed. There was no windows, no doors, no taps and no toilets in the houses. Because we never had a house and waited for so long, it didn't matter if it wasn't finished because we would complete it ourselves. When we got to the house, we all put our names on the houses. We moved into the houses as if it was our own. We felt at home.

We stayed in the houses for 2 months. On the 19th of February 2008 while we were still sleeping, we just heard whistles blowing and shouts of here comes the

Police, guns and oppression

boere [police]. We stand up and went outside. When we got outside the place was looking like a war field. In every yard there was one or two securities. Everywhere were police vans and caspers [armed vehicles] standing.

They told us that we must evacuate the houses. It was a very sad day. We all put our stuff like furnishers and stuff in the middle of the road. Some peoples stuff was put on a big truck and they went to dump the peoples stuff at warehouse in Blackheath. When they went to go look for their stuff, most of their stuff was missing, especially the expensive stuff like electronics and kettles and DVDs.

We were praying for a miracle to happen but there wasn't any mercy for us. The police shot rubber bullets at us because we were 'to cool and calm. They thought that because other people often throw stones at them, they thought that we also going to be violent. But we was always peaceful. I know about 20 people got shot including a 3 year old boy (who go shot 3 times). My child of 7 years old was in such a state that she cried and said she does not want to go back to the houses. It felt like I was in a horror movie or something. All of us was crying because we didnt have a place to stay.

That night we decided to move to the pavement. We slept under the moon and the stars. There was no roof over our heads. Thats where we're living now for almost 10 months. At first it wasn't easy to live like this. We all put us a hokkie [shack] to live in. We are now use to it and decided that this is where we were going to stay until we get our houses. Nothing else but houses. It was a long and cold winter here in the hokkies we called our homes. Our homes did leak in, we did sleep sometimes under wet blankets. Every second week my kids or me catch a cold. Sometimes we sleep then the raindrops fall on us. That was not easy but we survived. We on Symphony way are all very strong and survivors because other people went to the Blikkiesdorp because they couldn't stand the cold and the rain. They are all cowards. I put thumbs up for everyone here on Symphony way who is still here with us.

Here's only one tap and a lot of toilets here that more than 100 families must to use. Sometimes I got fedup of the pavement and the quarrels about children and big people who get in fights. But its not worse than there where I came from before we occupied the houses. I think by myself everything I went through and that I have no where to go with my family. We became very close to each other and felt that all of us here on the pavement are like one family. We are so used to live like fighting and quarreling. Here on the pavement we learn to forgive the people and live like a family.

One thing that is left from the struggle is a grandchild. Because here's no television or entertainment for the children. My daughter decided to do her own thing and fell pregnant. We heard that its going to be a daughter. I have decided to call her *Symphony* because she will remind us about the struggle. My husband turned 50 here on the road. I wont forget this struggle, I've never experienced something like this before. This is the first time that our people are fighting for something that we deserve. This makes us proud and thats why I want to name this child *Symphony*.

Valerie and Melvin Solomons

A children's Theatre of the Oppressed

A big family: the children of Symphony Way

We didn't lose faith in staying in the struggle

ON THE 19 February 2008 we've been evicted out of the houses. It was like watching a movie or making one, but the saddest of all was being evicted out of the houses you learn to love. Everywhere you looked was people struggling to get they belongings out of the houses because the police and trucks is coming to pick it up and go throw it on a open field. It was so sad to see the children crying and panicking, and then there was the police starting to shoot rubber bullets and there was people who did get hurt even children. They started shooting because people refused to clear the area. It was illegal for them to start shooting at us because the people were peaceful and were children and pregnant women all over the area. And then we didn't have a choice but to clear the area, the people was panicking because most of us didn't know where to go.

Later that day we decided to go to Symphony Way we the decided to all spent the night here. It was like laying under the stars. We took our blankets, planks, cardbox anything we can get hold of to make something to sleep under. No one actually sleep. Then the next morning everyone was in for the next step every 5 minutes we held meetings, we did get plenty of sponsors and so on. And then we decided we going to struggle here on the pavement in Symphony Way. So the next day people start building they hokkies [shacks].

Blikkiesdorp (backside), a bleak alternative for the Symphony Way Pavement Dwellers

And then of course there was people who decided to go to Blikkies and quick a lot of people was moving everyday. I was very amaze by some people who did move, we were 139 familys staying on the pavement and we one big family. Everyday heres something happening like for instants we did block the road so that cars can't ride here but theres always people who force and then we also can get very angry but we very nice and loving actually. At night or even during the day we make 'galies' [fires in small metal bins] to make food or to keep us warm. On weekends or during the week theres students coming from different places to come visit us. They learn the children how to use different objects like playing drums or taking photos or even playing games with them. We here on the pavement are one big Family and just hope to get our houses.

On the 10 September 2008 I did give birth to a beautiful baby girl and decided to stay here in my hokkie with my baby. Many people did say no you're baby will get sick or catch a cold but the winter is gone and she's still healthy and growing fast. Me and her father decided to give her the name *Hope* because we didn't lose Faith in staying in the struggle, no matter what she gave us more *Hope* to stay longer because our children's futures are at stake here. And now I'm closing my letter with love. Its just hope and love that motivates us to stay in the struggle. Thank you.

From,
Lee-ann Erasmus and the Erasmus family

These conditions are not for elderly people

I WAS ONE of the illegal occupants on the 19 December. I'm staying with my foster grandson and granddaughter Annelue. I'm staying with lovely people. Happy as everyone was, we were also evicted. That was the most horrible experience. Heart-broken and torn apart, I also moved to the pavement. My shack is not so stable and it leaks, but I have lots of friends who always help me as I am fifty-seven years old and every one young, old, and children calls me ouma [grandma].

Symphony Way has its little [vegetable] garden which I look after. I water it and even sew my own seeds. Tomatoes, gen-squash, sweet-melon, and other eat-able vegs grew in my little garden which keep me going. I'm a total bookworm and love everybody on the pavement. These conditions are not for elderly peo-ple, but my heart aches to have my own house before the creator take me to meet him. It not all sunshine and roses but this is the most memorable experience I will treasure. My only hope and reason for living is to have a house.

Cynthia Twigg

Survival and my Struggle

EVERYDAY ON SYMPHONY way is challenge. Life here feels like every day is the same routine, from sunrise to sunset we're struggling to cope with our circumstances. I battled to find something in this new life to challenge me and keep me motivated. It started when we moved into the N2 Gateway houses and then got evicted.

Before coming to live on Symphony Way, I felt empowered, like a home-owner, a owner of property. When my daughter woke up in the mornings, she woke up in her own room, as a member of a family she was proud to form a part of…she would happily say: 'Goodmorning Mammie, Goodmorning Daddy!'. I felt like a house-wife in charge of my own domain. From this, feeling like I was in my own home, is what was hardest to get used to.

I was pregnant with my child before we were evicted. A beautiful baby boy who was born on Symphony Way. I expected to give birth to my baby in this safe house that belonged to me, not on the pavement on Symphony Way.

For the last four months I have volunteered to help out at the crèche that the community of Symphony Way began to help the parents of children who have full-time jobs and no baby-sitter during the day. When I come to work in the mornings I feel challenged, that I have a purpose, that I am helping members of my community.

First thing in the morning we start the day off by making porridge, before the children eat we've taught them to pray. During the day, we teach them to sing, re-cite new nursery rhymes, draw, colour, those old enough learn to read and write. Being amongst these children daily helps me to change the way I think about the struggles in my life and concentrate on the good moments with the kids.

I hope next year we are in our houses, not struggling. Then we; my husband, my kids and I, can start a new life. I think every one would like to wake up in a house, not on the pavement.

Amanda Engelbrecht

Every child deserves a home

Here I've learnned

MY NAME IS Christabel Deeliah Small. I want to tell you about my experience here on Symphony Way. My personal experience is.

Firstly I would like to tell you what kind of women I was before I can actually start with my experience here on Symphony Way. I was a women that was only for myself when I had my first child nothing changed I was still the same. I had my second child & still nothing changed. I had all these different fears in me. So many fears that I didn't want to be alone. I got my strength from my children and with all these fears, I can face everyday. But back then, I only saw them weekends or maybe 3 to 4 times during the week because they were living there at my mother. When I had to face a problem and my children werent around, I was always running away from everything and everyone.

Until I came to live on Symphony Way. Here I've learned to face all my fears. The people that is living here with me on Symphony Way is friendly, loving,

caring, etc. All the things that I personally feared to feel because of my personal experiences in life. We share, we care, we stand together as one. Myself I wasn't a talketive person, now I speak to everyone that I know on Symphony Way even people that I don't know. I can also make friends now without being picked on. I can also ask without being shouted at. I can also help someone without being not thanked. Every night when we sit at the fire we talk, we tell stories, personal or even none personal. We crack a joke anytime when we like it.

I've also learned to make food on a fire, go fetch wood & make the fire all by myslef which I was scared of at first. Here I've learned to solve a problem before it started to get out of hand. Here I've even learned to compremize. Here I've learned to love. I've learned to speak my mind and not hold back. I've learned take responsibility for my own actions. I've learned give without receiving something or expecting something back. Here I've even learned to live without electricity. I've learned to make friends without even knowing it. I can cry without being talked about the next day. Here I've learned to interact with people that's even not from my culture or even my religion without being disrespected and disrespectful back.

With all the fears that I had in me I've learned to face them even when I'm alone. So my philosophy is don't let people make you do things that you don't want to do. Don't let them make or break you. Stand up for yourself when you don't like the things that someone else is doing or saying to you. Make yourself be heard. All these things I've come to learn in a small community & that is where I live now with my own family. So lets love one another & not make war.

This is all the small things that matter's in life & when I get my house I'm deffently taking my experience with me without leaving a single one behind.

Your faithfully
C.D. Small

To Whom it May Concern

MY NAME IS Bonita Seconds and I'm staying on the pavement on Symphony
Way. I'm the proud mother of two boys, Dwayne and Ashwin. Their father is
also with us. His name is Daniel Mathys. We are engaged to be married as soon
as we get our house. I just want to tell you about my family.

Dwayne is 6yrs old, my youngest, with the enquiring mind. He is so outspo-
ken and speaks whatever comes to mind. He will always ask questions about
anything, and he wants to be a builder one day. Because he wants to build houses for people.

Ashwin is 10yrs old and the shy one. He's a child who creeps into ones heart.
He dislikes to ask anything from people. You know they went through so much
in the past months. Especially Ashwin because I could see it in his school grades.
It was from Good to Bad to Worse. He didn't cope with what was happening,
the effect of the evictions was too big on him. I on the other hand didn't noticed
what was going on until I saw his grades in the third semester. I just pray to
God I wasn't to late to help him and that was what I did I helped him with his
homework.

When they are going to grow up, they must be something. They are going to
change something around in the world. So it is important. I myself didn't finish
school, but for them it is important to finish their school. We are just waiting on
his exam-report if he did pass. Now you see it was bad on him and I myself do
not wish this for any child.

It is so sad because I know I can't do anything about this problem we have.
Unlike the government who can do something about it but they don't care about
us here. Because if they was concern than we would have been in houses already.
I must add I was stunned when I heard the minister Whitey Jacobs say he was
Anti-T.R.A. (Temporary Relocation Area) because that was where we were suppose to go to by the City of Cape Town. I mean how can one live like that with
your children? What safety can you provide for your family? There is no safety
there and the structures they build with – the thieves, they just broke in there.
How can one bring your children up and guide your kids through that? That
is how little they think about us. I'm glad the minister said it about the T.R.A.'s
although I know that he was lying. But now he is obligated to provide us the
houses because of what he said.

You know we're in December now and it would be a blessing from God and
a special one if we can get our houses before Christmas. I mean it will be very
special because that is my dream and wish now for me and my family. I just
pray to God when the minister is making a decision for us that it comes from
his heart and not his mind. I also hope that God will give him the strength and

mindset to help us and listen to us. The other thing is, when we gonna get our houses, we on Symphony Way would like to have ours together and not one by one. We know each other by now. There is a bond now. The children know each other and play together. And I would like to stay near all of the people here on this road. Because we are a community now that wants to be together. I just wish the minister would understand it.

Thank You! Aluta Continua!

Bonita Seconds
Dwayne Seconds
Ashwin Seconds
Daniel Mathys

PS – It is a few months later now, and both of my children did pass their exams. I am very very happy for them – I even cried.

Living on the Pavement: My Life on Symphony Way

BASED ON A True Story

My name is Mina Mahema and I'm living on Symphony Way in Delft. As I am sitting and writing this letter I am just now thinking about my son who is so far away from me in Worcester, a little town in the Western Cape. Wondering what he is doing now and what is he thinking about his mother, I always use to tell him everything that I'm doing and going through is for him. I always use to hope that he had to understand. Everytime I see him he ask me did you already get the houses and I never know what to answer. I try to paint a picture for him that it is not to bad here on the road. Sometimes he is worried about me, am I warm or cold enough? I always use to tell him my child it is better than to live here than under someone else's roof, constantly need to be told when you must sleep, eat and walk around. For his eleven years of age on this earth he would answer me very politely, *then I understand your sacrifice mommy*.

I am also glad that he did not have to go through the same trauma that the other children have to go through when we were evicted out of the houses that we eligally invaded. That was under demand and order of one of our councellors FRANK MARTIN. He is part of the organisation called the D.A. That stands for DEMOCRATIC ALLIANCE. The day of the eviction he forsake us and we were guided and supported by an organisation called the ANTI-EVICTION CAMPAIGN which was led by ASHRAF CASSIEM and DELFT ANTI-EVICTION committee. When I think of all of this my thoughts become more cheerful thinking that for some things I am not sorry that I am on this pavement. Like for instance there was a lot of good things happening here. Children becoming active in sports and children being born on this road. Couples getting married and people falling in love.

Like I have met the love of my life on this road. Maybe I should start by how I met my prince charming. When I came on the road I just saw this guy up and down in the road. He use to be friends with an older man that was staying two shacks from ours. He was very loud and 'deurmekaar' meaning he was always in trouble. But for some reason I was not afraid of him like everybody else. He was aquainted with my older sister and thats how I met him. We first talk at the karaoke that was on the road. He ask me for a dance. The night was good and went well. The next day he invited me again to the next dance. That did not work out because we never got to the dance so we ended up sitting and socializing with other friends. Every body went home and we ended sitting the whole night throug. That is where it all started. I must say he is younger then me but

sometimes it feels like his mindset is so much more broader than mine. He always gave me the idea that he is more experience than I am. He could teach a lot of things that I did not know. I always use to say I am looking for a man that can only love me and respect me for who I am and more. I knew I had got that man but with a few sacrifices. Like for instances, he use to live a gangster life and always be on the wrong side of the law. I tried my utmost best to get him away from that and at times I succeeded. Until he began to have a jealous rage. He has decided that I am having an affair with one of my neighbours on the road. Wich I plenty of time try to convince him that it is not so. He could get furious when I would tell him that it is not so. At one time he took a trip to Joburg. He phoned me from Joburg and tell me that he heard that there is a man with me. Wich I denied because it is not the truth. That put him over the edge. That is where the verbal mental and sometimes physical abuse started. Up to this day where I have decided that I had enough and packed my things.

But I am still in that relationship of uncertainty. Other people would think, *now why stay in this abusive relationship*. And I would say that it is not a matter of wanting to be abused, to me personally, I wanted justification for myself. Maybe he used to do this in his previous relationships and he always came out the winner, but I wanted to show him otherwise. I always told him, that I might not be a university graduate, but am educated enough up to a certain level to help myself get out of different situations. He might want to say something and me, in this case, might just have to obey. But then I always tell him that I am not stupid, you can rather kill me but I will never agree to something that I am not satisfied with. I will not let him control me.

A part from that I have come to learn how to be proper and professional. Because we as a community sometimes had to attend meetings concerning our housing situation. I learned how to conduct myself and how to address my fellow comrades. Things that I have never knew like for example certain rights that I have as a citizen of this country and how you can protect those rights. We as the community took it upon ourselves as to even form a night watch to patrole at night. Because at the time we had to do something to protect ourselves and our children. Each family use to get a chance to patrol at night... A lot of things had happened here like one night we went to a photo exibition that potrays the struggle from the beginning until now. There was educators and inspirational speakers. We had a lot of visitors here on the road from foreign countries. There was also the churches that helped us with food and some organisations with clothing. Me personally, I became a member of a big family here on the road. I just want to spesify by saying I have met Bonita while I am here on the road and we became close friends and antie Florrie that is like a mother and of 'cause Evelyn who is like a big sister. What ever turn this struggle takes I will never forget these people and what I have learn.

I am closing this letter with good thoughts of every body that I have mentioned.

I carry this out to my son KEENO ANDREW MAHEMA

Love,
Mina Mahema

We won't tolerate any violence in our road

THIS WHOLE STRUGGLE for houses in Delft was started by the DA [Democratic Alliance] to get more Coloured votes into Delft because they knew that the 70% squatters and 30% backyarders would mean that there would be more Xhosas in Delft and they (the DA) would loose their wards in Delft. They started this invasion to mislead the people and they planned this whole thing so Blikkiesdorp would be formed and there would be more Coloureds in Blikkiesdorp coming from other squatter camps that have the majority of Coloureds. They are fetching backyarders from other areas like Elsies River, Hanover Park, Belhar, and Woodstock so they can improve their vote count in Delft.

They have caused and are causing racist tensions between the Cape Coloureds and the Black Africans because they were part of the allocation of houses (N2 Gateway). Thats why they saw that there are going to be more Black Africans in Delft and thats why they started the invasion and moving people from other places into Delft.

Once we were evicted from the houses, we as the community of Delft Symphony made a decision and a commitment in the beginning of the struggle on the 19th of February 2008 that we won't tolerate any violence in our road. Any person being violent or breaking into other people's places will be removed from our struggle for houses. That night, on the 27 of March 2008, Elmarie Isaacs and boyfriend and Brother John Jensen with his sons came with their pangas [machetes], knives and a gun to assault Aunty Jane [Roberts] and the committee on Delft-Symphony. The community made a decision to remove them and their property from the road. After the community removed them from the road, me and Riedewaan was accused of malicious damage to property.

I was sentenced to 6 months in prison on the 2 July 2008 for something I didn't do. I was exspecialy disappointed in the Judge when he told me and Riedewaan Isaacs (the other comrade and co-accused) that he is sentencing us in the *interest* of the community but the whole incident of removing Elmarie Isaacs and Brother John was done in the *interest* of the community. But the Judge didn't take that in to consideration and I wasn't even involve in the incident. But in the interest of the community and the struggle I accepted it.

I stayed for 2 months and 2 weeks at Goodwood Prison and was moved to Pollsmoor Prison for 2 weeks and was released on parole on the 2 October 2008 under house arrested until 01-01-2009 till my sentence is finish. This was my first time in prison which was very hard for me to accepted in the first 2 weeks that I was in prison but after that with the support of the Western Cape Anti-Eviction Campaign and the community of Delft Symphony, with my family, I accepted it. There was lot of things going thru my mind about our struggle for the poorest of the poor and I came to the conclusion that this government don't give a damn for the need of the poor because if this was somebody rich and/or a government official, he wouldn't have seen the entrance of prison.

One thing that made me very strong in prison is that I refused to give up my fight for the poor. I salute the Anti-Eviction Campaign for their struggle for the poor and thru God's grace I believe we will win our struggle for proper houses for the community of Delft-Symphony.

When I was on parole, I was told that I must not work for the Anti-Eviction Campaign anymore. But I dont work for Campaign, I do it voluntarily and no-one will stop me to fight for our right as citizens of our land South Africa. We were press down in the old regime and it is time that our voices as the Poorest of the Poor are heard. I will stay by our slogan that says No Land No House No Vote until we are heard in our country. I salute the Western Cape Anti-Eviction Campaign.

Now people can see what is politicians doing to the poorest of the poor. They are misleading them to stay in places that is not conducive for human beings (Blikkiesdorp). They are campaigning now for votes and making promises left, right, and centre, and they know that they can't keep those promises. After the elections, they will just forget about our poor. Seeking eviction orders, cutting down peoples water supplies, demanding that they take the water meters and that is against our human rights. And they as politicians forget about this.

Thats why I wont give up the fight to fight for our poor.

Aluta Continua. Our Struggle Continues.

They as the government can send me to jail again but they won't break my spirit!!!

Jerome Daniels

My Story

I, MNCEDISI SHAUN Plaatjies, would like to tell you a story as a resident of Delft-Symphony. We were in need for a house and I did the application for a house and I was given a card as proof that I'm on the waiting list of the housing department. Since we were in need for a house, one day a Councillor named Frank Martin told us to occupy the N2 Gateway houses because they were empty. So I for one was in need for a house. So I went for a house and I occupied the house on the 19th of December 2007. Most of the people that where in need for a house occupied the houses and we stay for about two months. After that, they filed an eviction for us which took place on the 19th of February 2008. Most of the people, men women and children, where evicted out of the houses like we where dogs.

It was a disaster for me and my family. Most of the people lost their furniture and their dignity as human beings. Our children ware trometised by the bull dozers and the law inforcement who call themselves the South African protective force. They are surposed to protect us but insted they treat us like dogs, they thru tear gas, rubber bullets, shouting at the people with children involve not having a heart and decency to at least evict us in a decent way without violence. The day was long as we had to move out of our houses, infact houses that we made our homes.

To me its painful, because my kids didn't deserve to be humiliated and disrespected the way our own people did. We look up to the policemen and whatever is happening to the community, we go report it to them. Going to the police, would be an insult to me, after what they have done. For me, its better that I sort out my problems myself. If I cannot sort it out on my own, I will got out to my community and ask them for advice or help instead of the police.

We squated on the pavement that nyt just a few yards from the houses that we where evicted from. That night is a day-nyt that I will never forget, because our families where our main concern and we had no-place to go, so we lay all nyt awake. To me most people on the road became my friends and family. That nyt, I thought about the situation that our four fathers were in, like history was repeating itself. Our Granies and Ootatomkhulu (Grandfathers) went through this. Ngoku, sithi kutheni, senzeni kwisizwe nakubantu esithi sibathembile bangabameli bethu besizwe sethu uMzantsi Africa (Now, we are saying what happened to *them*, what have we done to the country and to the people that we trust and look up to, who are in charge in South Africa)

The next day we started to build amatyotyombe [shacks] and we made a commitement that we will love, respect and protect each other till the day things turn out the best. To that promise we as the people squating at Symphony way commited our self to fight for houses till every one of us get a house, because we do deserve houses. What happen was that the where two people ie Ashraf Cassiem and Jane Roberts who are from the Western Cape Anti-Eviction. They offered to lend us a hand because they where hurt and they couldn't watch their own Nation be treated like that. Their work is helping people that are evicted and wrongly treated by their own people ie emphasise people rights and teaching them how to do things and how to be someone strong and how to relate to other people. We, as residents of Symphony, elected our own members and leaders, ie people that where committed and dedicated of helping and listening to peoples wants and needs. A committee was formed and we spoke as one. We were introduced to the responsibilties of being acountable for what we decide and for what we do and say to our community. We started having meetings with everyone and most of them was always at 18:00pm each and every day. We then sorted our differences and we kepted our promises and our mandate that we are all here for houses and we shall respect, honour, love and stay together no-matter what happens in the near future. Days, nyts went by. We started patrolings at nyt because of our safety. It was like to me, I'm introduce to a new world of which I thought I could not be. In the old communities, we had our differences and we didn't speak about them. Mostly, we didn't care about the other person – like my neighbours. Here we are together and united as one as a community. Most people got to know each other through the patroling duties because everyone had to participate including the women.

We, the resident staying on Symphony road, share each and everything we have. To us, the life here is not easy and simple but we are people; we believe that where there is a will there's a way; in god we believe; in one-another we trust. We are ordinary people on Symphony way, whatever we do, we do it together.

In our country, ie South Africa, we speak of 15 years of freedom, we all speak of Children rights and Women Rights, but truly and honestly they abuse those rights they speak and write about for our people We are trying each and everyday to gain/redeem our dignity and do what is best for our children because they don't deserve to be in this kind of invoroment. Its not good for them at all.

We started having marches to Thubelisha [Homes] (that is the company that is involve with the N2 Gateway Houses) and to Trafalgar (who was letting the people rent in Langa in the new N2 Gateway flats). People must be united as one because we need to stop what is going on in our country ie Rich people become richer and poor become poorer and not leting histroy repreats itself. If we can't do it for ourself, we can't let our children go throu what we are going throu. They are the key to the future.

We are people and we will stay people because god created us for a purpose. What I'm saying people lets stand together and unite, because we are the government, we are the world, what more could we not do if we are united as one? We are strong where we are on Symphony way and we make sure our kids are safe and enjoy each day of their lives with happiness. Even though the law inforcement comes and intimidate us and do damages to some-homes, we fight with love and let our kids not be scared, because when they see these policeman they runaway like they see death. Most of all we teach them that there is good in people no-matter what they do or say. Ndifuna ukuthi qinani maComrade isende lendaba (I just want to say, stay strong Comrades, this road ahead of us is still long) and Aluta-Continua. We shall strive for houses till the day that we are located to our houses. Qina mhlali ubambelele kwimpumelelo, ekunyamezela ukho umvuzo (Strength to the residents and hold on to success, at the end of the struggle there will be a positive outcome).

To me it seems history is repeating itself, it was our four fathers, now us, then tommorow it will be our kids. It can't go-on like this. We should have a heart for all. Thanks-may the lord bless you and keep us safe at all times.

Viva! Amandla ngawethu [power to us]!!!

The End

Mncedisi Shaun Plaatjies
Symphony Way
Delft
7100

We deserve a house!

I'M SARITA JACOBS with four sons and a husband. Together we're a big family with a big need. Sometimes life has challenges that are exciting and others are not, but what lies behind us are tiny matters compared to what lies within us. That led me to some poetry phrases:

Never have we expected that we shall ever regret by taken an unlawful action;
Lead by someone in a higher section.
A councellor supposed to help us,
but only causes mistrust.

Confusion and frustration becomes our tool to fight with integrity against the high authorities. We use our rights and powers to interpret our anger which pours like showers.

Here we are on Symphony Way;
We trust and so we stand,
to obey the rules and principles that an abandoned and misleaded community lay.
Together we shall stand, that's the mandate and a powerfull band;
Between each one of us and we are so committed in the presence of Him,
Our Guiding Hand…

Believe me or not, we will succeed
And we will help others with the very same need.
We truly deserve a house,
Me and my spouse;
Cause we are human and feel the sorrow
And still have hope for tomorrow.

Trials kept us strong
And we stand all along.
We know we have stumble,
But our failure made us humble.
Just the thought of leaving into our homes,
Brings happiness that keep us sweet;

I can assure you indeed.
The success so far, keeps us glowing
And we believe God keep us going!!!

The Struggle

Sacrifices

Trials

Reality

Unity

Goal

Grief

Love

Endless

S.T.R.U.G.G.L.E —> break it up in portions and meanings and according to my experience and understanding of the word I am writing these facts:

We live in upsetting and challenging times. Old values are replaced with new ideas, that which was regarded as wrong is now considered to be correct. Because of changing circumstances, age old traditions suddenly ask for a new approach. When you determine the value of the point of view which you are supporting you find these were the struggle that we now still are in which previous comrades has participated. Others has died and others found success. I whatsoever has been negligent and uninvolved for years and now you are suddenly challenged by a new thing. My opinion of this struggle is not to tell everyone everytime about the bad and inconvenience on this road, but to emphasise the facts and values that I have gained by which I can enrich many individuals to change and succeed! Reality look us in the face. We experience things we never have dreamed of. On the pavement, evicted from these houses opposite us, we gain strength and integrity. Powerfull acts such as the occupation of this road, not to go to a temporary relocation area, know your rights, refuse that authorities confuse and brainwash us in what you believe in, suffer by our actions… The pleas of our children: 'when are we getting houses?' Promises made that must be answered. Through all this my dignity never fade or dissappear. Make food on the Fire, making Firewood, use Gas, Parrafine stoves, Light candles, carrying Water in buckets… All changes that make us stronger. To the children it is fun and exciting. I often remind them that this is not the way it should be. Enjoy it as part of the struggle; think of it as a lesson whereby you can teach other children that life needs to be appreciated; not very smooth and comfortable, but through these challenges we will prosper. I have learned that you should have motivating powers that should drive you to fullfill your dreams or your goals. If the drive in your life is strong enough, you will be able to achieve your objectives at all times. It is however necessary to be still before God and think about the goal you set for yourself in life. Then ask yourself: Once I achieve this goal, will I really enjoy the deep satisfaction I have been yearning for? Will I enjoy true peace of mind when actually getting it? Because most people feel that at the end of a journey they have achieved little simply because they were driven by the wrong motives. The only power that can help you focus on the real values of life is the wisdom which is granted by God. I have learned that thoughts, wether it is inspiring or depressing, flashes through our minds and if we don't pay attention it controls our mind. Some thoughts weaken our character. I also learned that one must never play-act, but be yourself. In all of this you must not forget who you are. You cannot always plan life to satisfy yourself. You must make space for things that you didn't dream of to happen. Often we stood before the eyes of the law and its enforcements. People who should serve and protect the community. Many times they treat us like animals. They approach us in a rude and heartless manner. They intrude in our freedom; disrupt us in our privacy. Traumatise our children and weaken us mentally. They often causes our songs of joy to fall in our hearts for a moment, but our spirit then starts building up again as we realise what our goal on this road is: Fighting for houses!

It is a pity that so many people refuse to realise that love involves far more than a sentimental emotion. Genuine love goes deeper than this. You must be tollerant and understanding, sympathetic and support others. I will never forget where I came from and where we are now. I will never again look over others in need, in confusion, who has no where to go; people struggling but not knowing how to reach. Soon we will be in our own houses with our very own privacy where we can emphasise and practise what we have learned as a family on a solid floor, helping us in the growth and education of our children. Let us no longer complain about how full of grief life is. No eye has seen, no ear has heard, no mind has conceived what God has prepared for those who love Him. I experience that your loved ones becomes more dearer to you, your friendships become more closer, how to greet becomes more important and meaningfull, to give to those who don't have, to share tears and joy together United we shall stand – that is our mandate.

I have learned that real comrades suffers an injustice themselves, rather than allow the community to be exposed. I even learned that Toyi-Toyi is not just a dance, but a protest which happen when people are not happy about their circumstances or want to force their concern in the public, hoping that the authorities will adhere to them or do something about it. Participation, unity and communication forms part and parcel of this struggle which make a powerfull impression on high authorities and others in similar situations who never thought of doing things we does to change their circumstances.

It is not always good that everything thats inside of you must come out because it does not always have positive results because what is inside of you is not always to the advantage of those hearing it. Here we are also beware of dead ends. You feel sometimes life has no meaning. Even your spare time makes no difference to this coulourless routine. Such an attitude, I experienced is totally unnessecary. Even so you allow yourself to become a victim of this apathetic attitude to life, instead of set-

tling for a constructive meaningfull lifestyle. The struggle encourage me to make it happen. I had to gave up certain things in order to gain more and better; to discover the values and meaning of life as such. I had to forget about myself and strive for what I really want and not thinking about the consequences thereafter. The result at the end will be more rewarding and you will appreciate life in full. Me and my family deserves a house. We have discovered values that we must live out in full in the comfort of our own house. We are human. We have dreams. We have morals. We have expectations. Victoriously we will share them with the world. That entitle me to speak like Jacob in the Bible: 'I will not let you before You bless me.'

My sincere appeal to those who opress us. Stop robbing people from living their lives as human beings with affordable living in a decent environment.

The struggle continues and so my knowledge grows. Thank God for what I'm part of that made me a better person!

Aluta Continua! Amandla – Awetu.

Sarita, Nigel, Kurtly, Shane, Charl and Gabriel Jacobs

Ons 'bly of gly' huis

MY NAAM IS Nicolene Manewel en ek was een van die N2- Gateway besetters.

Op die 19 Febuarie 2008 was ons ge-evict uit die huise wat ons beset het, daai dag was alles deur mekaar, want ons het nie geweet wat te kant toe nie.

Ons het al ons besittings na die pavement gedra. Ons het besluit om in Symphony Way te plak, en daai aand het ons almal in Symphony Way geslaap en dit was 'n groot uitdaging, want dit was koud en winderig en ons het enige iets gebruik om 'n skuiling te maak teen die koue en winderige weer. Ons was soos 'n groot family want ons gesinne het somer vuur gemaak en gesels. Ons het daai nag geoorleef. Die volgende oggend was alles deurmekaar en dit was baie moeilik om aan te pas om weer te hervestig op 'n different manier. Daai oggend toe moes ons onsself was met 'n T-shirt en afdroog met koerant papier, maar ons staan nog sterk. Ons structure was twee mattrase wat ons tussen in geslaap het, maar soos die tyd aangegaan het, het ons vir onsself 'n beter structure gemaak met balke en seil en ook enige eits wat ons kan kry om dit geskik te maak. Ons woning se naam is Bly of Gly no. S 79. Bly of Gly beteken ek bly nou hier, wanneer ek hiervandaan gaan ek na my huis. Ons woon nou al een jaar op Symphony Way.

Ons het baie dinge geleer op Symphony Way Bv. Om mekaar te respect en om geduldig te wees, soos hulle sê als gebeur nie oornag nie, alles vat tyd. Maar ons weet ons struggle nie verniet nie, net vir 'n huisie vir my familie want ons het al by baie mense gebly en voel net ons kinders raak groot en verlang ook 'n huis met 'n agterplaas van hul eie.Ons sal nooit vergeet wat ons alles moes deur gemaak het hier op Symphony Way. Nie vir Wat nie? Net vir 'n huis vir my en my twee kinders (dogtertjies) en ons vertrou net opdie Here (ons maker) Amen.

Nicolene Manewel

Our 'Stay or Go' house

MY NAME IS Nicolene Manewel and I was one of the N2 Gateway settlers.

On the 19th of February 2008, we were evicted out of the houses that we invaded, on that day everything was chaos, nobody knew which way to go.

We carried everything to the pavement. We decided to stay on Symphony Way and that night we all slept on Symphony Way and that night was a big challenge because it was cold and windy and we used anything to get some shelter. We were like one big family, we made fires to keep us warm, have jokes and fun. That night we outlived the cold. The following morning everything were in chaos and it was difficult to fit into this different manner of life. That morning we had to dry ourselves with a T-shirt and newspaper but it only made us stronger. Our structure was two mattresses that we slept in between. As the time went on, we made a better structure made with [wooden] battens, a plastic sail, we actually used anything we could get a hold of. We named our home Bly of Gly [Stay or Go] no. S79. Bly of Gly means I stay here now, when I leave here I am going into my house. We have now been staying here for a year on Symphony Way.

We learned a lot on Symphony Way for example: to respect each other and be patient, like they say everything don't happen overnight, everything takes

Give me a home: Symphony Way families demonstrate together on Stellenbosch Arterial exactly one year after they occupied Symphony Way

time. But we know we don't struggle for nothing, just for a house for my family because we lived at many people's backyards and we feel that our children are growing and is also longing for their own house with their own backyard. We will never forget what we went through here on Symphony Way. Not for what? Just for a house for me and my two children (my little girls) and at this moment we only trust in God (our maker), amen.

Nicolene Manewel

Ongetitled

VOLGENS MY EKSPERIMETERING om op die pad te bly was vir my 'n mees gewildste ervaring van my lewe, want dit het my hele lewe op stilstand gebring.

Dit was nie meer vir my 'n plesier om skool toe te gaan nie, want terwille van die feit dat daar nie elektrisiteit is nie kon ek nie my skool klere stryk nie. Ek het min tyd in die oggende terwille van die elektrisiteit omstandighede. Om met ongestrykte klere skool toe te gaan was vir my 'n verleenteid. As gevolg van al die omstandighede moes my ouers my uit die skool in Delft uithaal en in Eerste Rivier by my tante sit, daar is die omstandighede meer gemaklik. Steeds is dit nie 'n uitweg nie, want om by ander mense te bly mis ek my ouers [wat op Symphony Way bly].

My ouers se werk en geld omstandighede het baie verander. My moeder se gesondheid omstandighede het ook baie agter uit gegaan as gevolg van haar suiker, hoe bloeddruk, niere en hart. Gedurende my eksamentyd kon ek nie konsenteer nie, want ek het in die klas elke dag gewonder is my ouers veilig in die omstandighede waar hulle noe in bly in Symphony Way want dit is baie koud en die hokkie waar hulle in bly lek en is baie onveilig. My vader het sy werk ook verloor, dit is wat my baie getref het. Nou is ek bekommerd oor my skoolloobaan en toekoms, want ek wou graag universiteit toe gegaan het.

Ons soek maar net 'n huis waar ons as 'n familie kan saam leef. My ouers is op 'n waiting list al vir twaalf jaar.

Ons het nou hier op Symphony Way geen vryheid nie.

So Mr. Government, ek vra net 'n huis. (Sandonique Schultz). Minister, wat verhoud ons om huise te kry ons bly naby die bosse. Die rotte en muise eet ons se kos. Dis is iriteerend. Die Law-enforcment wat ons so uit kom gooi, ons hokke somer netso enige tyd in die nag en dag afgooi. Hulle kom net om ons se hokke af te gooi, maar hulle kom nie om "crime" toe te pas en ons te beskerm nie.Ons is nie diere nie, want dit is hoe hulle ons behandel. Ons verdien ook om in 'n gemaklike huis te woon net soos u. Meneer [Government] gaan lekker Kersfees hou met lekkernye en kos en ons moet sand kos eet. Gin ons ook asseblief 'n dak oor ons kop wat lekker warm en gemaklik is. So dat ons kos kan eet wat sandloos is, asseblief maak u hart oop vir ons . Die Here sal u seën.

Van: *John Schultz (Daddy) Pa*
Jeniffer Schultz (Mommy) Ma
Sandonique Schultz (Daughter) Dogter, ouderdom 16
Symphony Way
Delft

Untitled

FOR ME, TO live on the road, was for me a very wild experience because my life come to a whole still stand.

It wasn't, for me, a pleasure to go to school anymore because of the fact that there isn't electricity to iron my clothes for going to school in the morning. I got little time in the morning because of the conditions of electricity. It was very disgusting for me to go to school with un-ironed clothes. Through these circumstances, my parents had to take me out of the school in Delft and put me in Eerste Rivier by my aunt, because the conditions is more better there. Although it is not a solution to stay by other people, I still miss my parents [who live on Symphony Way].

My parents work and money conditions has changed a lot. My mother's health condition has gone backwards because of her different sicknesses like high blood pressure, sugar diabetic, and kidney and heart problems. During my exams I can't concentrate because of the conditions my parents stay on Symphony Way, due to their safety, cold and leakage of the hokkie [shack]. My father also lose his job and that was affecting me. Thats why I was a little bit worried of my schooling and future because I was planning to go to university.

All that we want is just a home for our family where we can live together. My parents are on the waiting list for 12 years.

Now we've got no freedom on Symphony Way.

So Mr. Government, I'm (Sandonique Schultz) just asking for a house Minister, what keeps us from having a house because we stay nearby the bush. The rats and mice are eating our food. This is very much irritating. Anytime during the day or night, the Law-enforcement just come throw our hokkies down. They just come and throw down our hokkies, but they are never there to stop crime and to protect us. We are not animals, but that is the way they treat us. We also deserve to stay in comfortable houses like Mr [Government]: you can have a lovely Christmas and to eat lekker [tasteful] luxuries and food but we must eat *sand-food*. Just please give us a roof over our head that is comfortable and warm and easy for us to live in. So that we can eat food without sand, please open your heart. God will bless you.

John Schultz (Daddy) Pa
Jeniffer Schultz (Mommy) Ma
Sandonique Schultz (Daughter, 16 years) Dogter
Symphony Way
Delft

You can light your candle when you want to

HI, MY NAME is Nicholas Reynolds. You see, I have got 4 children named Clayton, Branden, Matthew and Leeroy. My wife is Desiree.

I am on the waiting list since 1987, the 24th of the 3rd month. Thats 21 years. So I was thinking that at the time when I went to go apply for the house, that the city council and the local government would see my application to give me a house for me and my family, but nothing has happened like that.

Afterwards, I have had to 'put my neck-in' to other people's yards with my family. So many times have I been to the city council to ask them: how far is my application now? But everytime that I come there, then they always have got an excuse that they are busy with the years 1985 or 1986, so I have to wait till they came to 1987.

When we move from this backyard to the next backyard all your furniture is getting spoiled and broke. So, the reason why we have to move from one backyard to the next backyard is because of the owners from the house getting in arguments with your children (because there is always fights with the owner's children and my children). Because it is their house, that is why your children are always on the 'wrong' side. Sometimes when they get in fights with your wife or children, they lock the doors and then you wife and your children must ask the neighbors to use their toilets and ask them for water to drink. You buy electricity but when they get in arguments with your family, they pull out the plug and you have to go without electricity even though you buy electricity. Sometimes people charge you 750 to stay in their backyard. When the time just kills me staying in people's backyards, I go to rend a home. I ask the people to pull a legal lease up, but then they say no we must just do it verbally. Then when they have got a lot of money out of you, they decide you must empty the house because they are going to put other people in. The reason why they can tell you this is because they didn't pull up a legal lease.

And after all that, I decided to go and buy a house through the bank and the bank gave me approval for the bond from 86,000 Rand. Then they put the deal on hold because the owners still owe the city council too much.

After this deal goes through the mat, I found myself and my family in the N2 Gateway when we occupied those houses here. Then we were evicted out of those houses. Now I stay on Symphony Way with my wife and my 4 children. At least here on Symphony Way weve got freedom here because there's no people or owners to from the houses to say your children can't play here or can't play there; because there is no one who can lock the doors and say you can't use the toilet or the tap. And theres no one who can pull out the plug to leave you in the dark, because here where we stay now on Symphony you can light your candle when you want to.

When we move from Symphony Way, we would like to move into our own houses – but not shack. Otherwise we will stay on this road until they will give us houses, Because we will not go back to backyards, because we have our freedom now until we are going to get our houses – then we will have more freedom.

They say theres children's rights. By the time they evicted us, they take the children's rights away along with our human rights.

So now I want to know, what will the government do about this? Because I am waiting for 21 years for a house and if I look around in this N2 Gateway, theres youngsters from 18/19 years old who've got houses here. I would like to know how old they were when they applied for a house.

I tire now from waiting.

Nicholas Reynolds

I choose to take a stand

THE BASIC IDEA is that everybody here is looking for houses. Many people still see it as a government issue. The mandate from the people when this new government was elected was based on the Freedom Charter where it was said and undertook that there shall be houses, freedom and prosperity. That became a constitutional issue when the new government came into power. In the constitution the right to basic housing was enshrined, not as a luxury but as a right.

If I ask myself what I can do to change the situation I will have to overcome my own inhibitions. I will have to take myself to the war and not allow the war to come to me. I will have to ask myself how am I going to engage this issue. What can I do to take the struggle to a level to ensure that these goals can be achieved.

We want secure housing for our children. We looking at second and third generation of families. Whatever we do today will be a statement for the second or third generation children.

Passive resistance is another form of struggle, another form of fight. When you distance yourself from the struggle you waiting for someone who can lead you, to show you or teach you what this fight is about. That will be the time when you have to ask yourself am I prepared to step up to the plate and make it a reality.

The broader struggle will be continuous. For as long as there is a democracy in this country, the struggle will be continuous. The goals of the broader struggle would be to just listen to the need of the people and facilitate plans to always put new agendas forward from a political standpoint.

Because we are still a very far way off from a two party state. Because my view is basically is what I would like to see happen in this country is the leading party and a strong opposition. Because smaller and minority parties are still locked in a power struggle of this aim. Because if the goal of the people were to be honoured, let me choose that word, the movement of the country would shift from a multi-minority party state to a two part state with a strong opposition. I think the point about minority parties and a strong opposition that definitely detracts from the changes that can be brought about in a two party state with a strong opposition. There would be more finances and the people and the government level would ensure the right changes.

There will be many people who will say that the government failed them but the alternative is also there because if you look at the time when there was an apartheid regime, schooling was offered and every person had opportunity to choose schooling. Every person had the opportunity to change him or herself there. In the situation I am in I would be a second or third generation child from

previous dispensation. The education or thought that was created in the minds of my parents and grandparents would still have been relevant at this time when I was growing up and my thought pattern was developed.

I think first and foremost you must expose yourself to new ideas and allow other people to share their views on the same terrain, and if I don't speak to you, you would have a set idea of what might be happening but if we exchange views you can see the underlying facts, you can read between the lines but the underlying facts will still be there.

I choose to occupy, I choose to take a stand. What did I feel when I chose to move in here? I would have to say I have taken it as my right to have one of these houses. Technically that was undertaken. This is where it becomes more shades of grey than black and white. The councilor at that time made it a possibility to already proceed to that point. And many people were… some people might thought to be deceived, some people may think 'led to believe', some people might have thought it to be a reality that what I am supposed to have is gonna be mine. Many people were disillusioned. More devastating was when people were faced with the fact that we would be forcibly evicted from such houses in the presence of police. This brought people to the biggest confrontation they have ever experienced in their lifetime.

You must look at it from my point of view. I was a teenager back in 1976 when the struggle intensified. We were boycotting schools, we were throwing stones, we were physically, literally, overthrowing the government of the day. I've been shot at and I've been chased by secret police, I've had to physically make myself invisible in plain sight. That is why I say that this was a big change; confrontation with police. It's unreal; you will not be able to make the same decision, you will not be able to intellectualise any decision or thought afterwards, because you are under intense pressure at the time and your thought process would have been in shambles.

Disappointment was great for many of the people. If I will allow myself to go to a holding area it's like I'm going to prison when I haven't even been sentenced for a crime. For me it's like a P.O.W. camp. Initially if you look at how the whole TRA [Temporary Relocation Area] was erected, started, initiated. You would be blind open-eyed not to take glimpses of these things when you look at prison camps. Often here we are only catching news glimpses about the war and struggles in Europe. That the kind of images that came to my mind when I see the blikies [tin shacks]. Now I haven't spoken to many people who were prepared to speak openly about them. I cannot judge anything from hearsay.

The struggle is basically only the government's failure to provide at grassroots level our constitutional rights, which is a failure on your constitutional rights and if the government needs to be brought to book on the abuses then they ought to be taken to court.

It could come, but government time can take forever. There's this lady in Wallacedene, Irene Grootboom, she took the government to court. She won a landmark case. She never had the privilege to enjoy the fruits of her labour.

It begs the question: if we were fighting to overthrow the apartheid government of the day, can we truly say that the government is upholding the Freedom Charter on which the constitution was built?

Arnold Hendricks-Van Wyk

An ice-cold night. Delft is known for its extreme weather

Remembering the eviction of the 19th of February 2008, one year later.

Our sea of troubles here in Symphony way

'Ezekiel 36:16-38.' *When I make you clean from all your sins I will let you live in your cities again and let you rebuild the ruins.*

ONCE GOD HAS shaped us into the image he wants us to be, then he will put us back in our homes again because we did not deserve it before this.

It is not just a battle for a house but also a battle of your soul, drawing closer to God, having faith in God and making sure that your stand with God is right. At the end of it all, the way God used Moses to lead the Israelites threw the red sea is how he will use the committee and Anti-eviction campaign leaders to lead us threw our sea of troubles here in Symphony way.

Never did I think that My family would be a victim of eviction 1 day. All I could think of at that moment was; *What now? Where to from here?*

How do you explain to your kids that your next home is to be on the pavement. Maybe for a few days, weeks or even months or years. Maybe even for as long as the government feels like leaving you there. Living on a pavement is not an easy thing to make threw. You need patience, strength and you can only get that from God. With a community that sticks together and God in controlle of everything you can make it, you will make it. I never knew the things that lay ahead for this family but I knew with God on my side, I will make it threw my storm.

August 2008 my 3 year old daughter got burnt with hot water straight from a fire. Both her legs got burnt but my God healed her beautifully. When we had no money for gas, I would have to go into the bush for firewood. This road called Symphony way had it's own good and bad days that went with it. Hot water struck my family more than once, it struck 3 times. September 2008 my 11 year old Daughter got burnt with hot water. There too, God healed her beautifully.

At the end of September 2008, my children's room burnt down. By now I was angry, frustrated and hurting like never before. God knew why He allowed all these things to happen to this family because 1 thing is for sure, he carried us threw and these things really strengthened me as a mother, a wife and as a child of God. Waiting for a house in a hokkie [shack] on a pavement really taught me how to be patient. This was a test we were going threw and this is 1 test I am going to pass. I knew the harder it got the closer I was to receiving my house and that there was no way in hell that I was gonna give up the fight now. We want a house and we will receive a house from God.

Hot water struck again, only this time it was me. But I serve a miracle working God and the devil is liar because I did not have a mark on my leg. When we lived in the houses we weren't the people God wanted us to be. I was a 'so called christian,' and came on with the lord as I wanted to. But no more, God is my

no. 1 priority. If I'm on this road because God wants to trim me [like a hedge is trimmed and shaped] and wants me to be a living Testimony then so be it. My husband Conway, my 3 kids Dalana, Wesley and Nikita and myself Sharon Payn are still on this road 8 months later awaiting our house, a place where we can feel safe, a place my kids can call home. We've had sleepless cold rainy nights in this place and we've had happy times.

Thubelisha [Homes] might have powers, Whitey Jacobs might have the biggest say, But My God has the last say and the greatest Powers above all.

Sharon Payn

From the poor man to the rich man to conciliate the grounds of where we come from

PUT YOUR SHOES into my shoes and wear me like a human being would wear another human being.

I say to anybody, try for one night and sleep outside without a blanket, try for one night, you lawful people, to sleep outside without a blanket, try for one night and take your wife with you and your kids, and sleep outside without a blanket, without eating, and you'll feel exactly what it feels like to be in my shoes....

I was confused, scared, and disabled to maintain my family, in which, the only choice of decision that came to mind was to take the law into my own hands as the law has deprived me of my rights. In which it wasn't a simple step to take because I knew that there were consequences behind it that would jeopardize my family and, most importantly, my kids, the tomorrows future. Because of blatant promises of houses that were promised to us 15 years ago from when Mandela had taken the chair of the apartheid system in order to de-racialise it.

In which, the promises made are not are not fulfilled due to the economy and the corruption of the higher guys in the higher positions that are still provoking, undermining, and threatening to the underprivilaged people such as I. In which, it makes it impossible as a poor person to walk into a bank and ask to be finalised for a home loan due to the finances that we receive are to low a wage to maintain the banks' profits.

As a result, there we find ourselves in a situation of where we have to forcefully take on grounds that are not ours. Because if you look at other options to try to rent a house in which the rental in Cape Town is very high (nothing less than 1,600 rand in a backyard of where you do not have your own freedom and your children do not have a playing space for freedom due to the owners only require for your children to be in a specific area of within that backyard house of where they are not allowed to break or damage any property or else you will be held responsible for the cost of damages that your kids may have damaged).

Now, why I am on the way of Symphony Way is because even when I know that I have taken up space that belongs to the government, I know that the government owes me a home because he promised me that.

And not only that, but for the mere fact that I am free. I am free because I have choice, because I have opportunity, and mostly because I am suppressed in my position as a poor person.

The beauty of this place is when you see wrong being done you can go up to your fellow neighbour, in which your neighbour is your friend, your colleague, your supervisor, and your neighbour is also the law because we all fight for what is right. This is the feeling of being free. Ultimately you are free here on Symphony Way.

Try this and put a dog in a corner or an alley of where it does not have a way out but through you will be its only way of escape. I can bet you, that that dog will challenge you in its fearfulness that will become courage, and through faith, I assure you, it will pass you or else, most probably kill you.

Now why I say this? It is that you cannot, as a rich man, withhold me from my rights of having a home since seeing that you have promised it. Because then, if you hold back, then think of that dog and place me in that dogs position and I am human. I will by no doubt lash back and lash back hard because you are cornering not only me but the thing I love the most, my kids. Thats the best way to victimise a man and treat him like a dog in which I don't think that you want to be that person standing in his way.

The road that we live on, on Symphony Way. I finally came to terms of understanding pure nature. Reason being: snakes walk into my house and walk out of my house, freely. Scorpions, the same. And even more, the other animals that I have not seen yet with my naked eye, also have the freedom of my home that I now live. And the only way of survival is to understand nature. Now, its a life threatening and dangerous position for the rich man to live amongst such venomous and poisonous animals. But yet, my kids, and my fellow brothers and sisters and families of Symphony Way are living it to a reality. But yet still, we are underminded, interrogated, and frustrated by the outsider called the rich man that the law abiding citizens such as the SAP/SAPS that want to evict us from our freedom to put us into misery or something even worse than my freedom, like a shack in Blikkiesdorp.

Now who gives them the right to take our freedom of choice and happiness away from us instead of giving us houses and lock us up like dogs in a place we are not familiar with. Are they not asking for us to lash out in every way possible? To make them feel the same pain and anguish that we now are going through. Nevertheless, we are also law abiding citizens. But there's one thing I can say, that we, fight for what is right and not otherwise. That is why, we are here on Symphony Way, with choice. Because of what was promised to us years ago we are still waiting. Its insensible to take us from one shack and put us into another shack instead of a house.

Now, for the person that is wealthy, I'd say, that you are very high and mighty but you are very small-minded. As a result, I am not the fool you think I am to undermine me and make me want to live in a zinc shack. I am happy where I am and the only place I will move to from here on will be in the promised home that I deserve for my family and for the future that was promised to us as a new South Africa.

Viva South Africa! Viva! Make my dream become a reality and make me feel part of the new South Africa, the new millennium that we all speak of.

I am not a foreigner, nor an illegal alien, so I dont expect to be treated like one, that has no root and has no home (not that anyone should be treated that way that in turn makes you feel like a slave to someone else's country). And yet, I am a human being and each human being should be treated like a human being and not a slave.

Now for you rich people, lounging with the cat (the government) upon your lap, stretching out your slippers to the fire, and giving a sleepy yawn, and stating: *Oh Bother! Why are they living that way?* If for a moment, you put yourself into my shoes and for a moment of time come out of your warm position and visit me or even spend a day when it is raining in my hokkie, then you will feel the emotional distress of whereby I think that even you (the same person that I pay for through VAT) are likely to cry bitter tears because of the pain that you see of someone that doesn't want to be in this position but has no money to afford a better position. Someone that has a dream but because of suppression from the rich man makes it impossible for them to pull through that dream.

I think its because of shear selfishness. What I learned in the old days, that if you have plentiful, then you should give to the poor and you will be blessed in many ways. That it will overflow in many ways. That is why this world is so corrupt. Because the rich man has become so stingy and still wants to suppress the poor making it impossible for the poor man to survive on the little he has and that is why we are still here in waiting to fulfill that dream.

The rich man must let go of his wealth so that the week may become strong and a better nation for tomorrows future. Its called *sharing*. The simplest word you can find in the simplitic way of announcing. *Sharing* as a whole, bring a nation together as one. 'Ubuntu': *Umuntu ngu buntu wa bantu. Because a person is a person by people.* And we will all live in harmony because we are also human beings with understanding, initiatives, feelings, and dreams.

We have learned to know that patience is virtue and virtue is patient. In which we have patiently waited long enough. And in the struggle we have learned a lot by sharing with the families of Symphony Way. And uniting us together as one. One nation, one home, one vote. That has pulled us on this road so far and so long.

Luck tapped upon a cottage door.
A gentle quiet tap.
And Laziness who lounged within, the cat upon his lap
Stretched out his slippers to the fire,
And gave a sleepy yawn.
O Bother! he says, *let him knock again!*
But luck was gone.

Luck tapped more faintly still
Upon another door,
Where Industries was hard at work
Mending his cottage floor.
The door was open wide, at once.
Come in, the worker cried.
And luck was taken by the hand
And gladly pulled inside.

He still is there, this wondrous guest,
Whose out his magic hand,
Fortune flows fast you know,
But Laziness can never understand
How Industries found such a friend.

Luck never came my way, he sized.
But quite forgetting the knock upon his door that day.

This has been a feeling. When I feel. That I feel. I am going to feel a feeling that I've never felt before – by taking what is rightfully mine.

If only they will know now that our patience has run out. We can also divert and take what rightfully belongs to us. Our freedom of right to live in better homes because the rich man refuses to give. So the only best solution to solve this problem is to take back. Until the rich man can give, then the poor man can stop taking. But if he does not give, we won't stop taking until they feel our pain.

Its the same thing as example: we manufacture and make the bread. But if you are not going to allow us to have a piece of that bread that we make, automatically, we are going to be hungry and eventually we gonna look at bread so much, in our hunger, that we end up taking it. And we dont just take the least, we take the most because we have a family to feed as well.

So give me what I want, then you won't have to suffer the pain of knowing what I will do, when I do it, that I do best – taking what rightfully belongs to me. I learned it from you, the rich man. Where you have taken mine, and you have not brought it back. Limitedlessly, as Symphony Way, we have built up the courage, the strength, and the power, to take back what rightfully belongs to us.

This has really been the pain that has been bottled up and needs to be exposed. Its so traumatic, words are not enough to express it. Its a sad South Africa.

Sharing is necessary. It is because we have watched ourselves being robbed broad daylight in front of our eyes, that we have had enough.

Conway (in action with) Payn (on Symphony Way)

How the pavement changed our life

DAY ONE: LIFE on the pavement actually started the time it became dark. Sitting and thinking how our life changed in one day, from being happy in a house with no windows, doors, water, light and no bathroom. But one thing was for sure, we as a family were happy.

Then the unthinkable thing happened. Life on the pavement. The first night we hardly slept, everyone was sitting around, some were standing, some were patrolling, while some women and children were trying to get some sleep.

Next we learned how to build a structure. Never thought I would actually live in one but I did.

The first couple of weeks it was very frightening to sleep here because of the snakes, the insects, and we even learned to live with the flees. Children got sick, there was no hospital money, how did we get them right again? Yuh! We had to help each other out with medicine.

There was one night in the winter when it was time to get into bed and we actually got into bed. And the whole roof collapsed because the water was too heavy on the roof. Blankets were wet, clothes were wet, the bed was wet. We had to put on clean clothes that were wet. We had to get up and sweep out the water out of the hokkie [shack]. There was many nights where we had to lay awake because we had to monitor all the hokkies that were collapsing because there was a lot of single women with children. And most of the time we was scared to sleep, because of the wind, we thought the hokkies was gonna collapse on us.

Say about a week after that incident with the roof, I lost my job because I had to stay a lot out of work to build a better structure. Henry also lost his job as a car mechanic a couple of weeks after me. After that we had to eat pap/porridge in the morning, in the evening, the whole day. Because that was the cheapest food. Sundays, if we had a couple of bucks, we had to eat hoender netjies [chicken necks]. But still my children sayed *thank you – the food was very nice.*

Sometimes there was no petrol in the car and Henry had to walk from Delft to Mitchell's Plan. We even had to sell our mechanical tools and our fridge for food.

After picking up all the broken pieces, life began struggling to settle in. We had to learn to go to the bush to get wood to start a fire to cook food on, as well as using the sponsored toilets for washing lines, finding some material to secure your structure for the wind and rain, wlking for water everyday. Life on the pavement became more adventurous everyday.

Since that, we met a lot of different kinds of people and learned to respect different kinds of people and treat them the same way because we are in the same boat now. We had to respect other people because everyday we need each other.

Here on the pavement, my children also learned how to respect one another, share food, and they don't mess food anymore. Because they know if they mess, there is not food and no one to give them food, because this is all poor people on the road and lots of people lost their jobs like us.

This thing brought our family closer together.

Thinking back makes me wonder how we actually got here. I will never forget this part of my life.

I appreciate you taking time out of your busy life just to read this story and know what we went through.

Bonita Jubelin
(Kaylin, Cameron and Dowayne Jubelin and Henry Kammies)
S21 Symphony Way
Delft
7100

My Silver Lining

I AM SHAMIEL (Tillings) Mullins. Thank you for reading my story and I hope you learn something from it. I lived in Bonteheuwel for many years. And over the main road I saw a lot of shacks. Today I know why those people lived the way they did. I was always on the outside looking in and never knew what those people went through on a daily basis.

On the 19th February 2008 I met my husband on Symphony Way, Delft. This was the start of my experience on how people had to cope with life in the shacks. We were evicted in the early hours and had to struggle to get our belongings over the main road. All through the day it was very hectic and as night came we were only three women and a bunch of children in our family and we needed a warm place to sleep and a fire. The first obstacle (a place to sleep) the woman sorted out and the second (the fire) my 'now' husband provided.

We started talking and found that not only were we both the same starsign, but the same age give or take a week. Things got very interesting since we both have very strong personalities and similar views and as most of us know, this combination can give u *a lot of sparks without matches*.

He built me my first home (shack) and we got married two months after we met. As Muslims (just like in other religions) we felt it was a sin to sleep together out of wedlock. So, to set an example for our kids and because we love each other, we decided to get married sooner rather than later.

Now, after a year living on Symphony Way, I can see why those people went through what they did. I dont think that anybody who has got an option, would be living in shacks or on the street because you have to go look for water. Its not like you can go to the toilet and flush the toilet or just open the tap and get water. You have to stand in a line to fill bottles and carry them long distances. You have to deal with spiders and scorpions and snakes on a daily basis. Its not something that you learn how to deal with unless you experience it firsthand.

I feel ashamed to think that once I thought that shackdwellers were being unnecessary and that they were just seeking attention. Now I know better and feel I owe most of them an apology for being so stupid and judgemental. Today I am also living the same way as them and being looked at in the same way that I looked at them.

Now I have realised that its not easy to get what you want and live a life thats complete if you dont have your own home. We may live in a shack, but we try to set good examples for our kids and show them that even though life is hard, you can still do the best you can and not loose hope. We may live in a shack, but we have a home. With the help of God 'Allah', we will soon have a house so we can have our own piece of Freedom.

To all those people living in shacks I say to you *Aluta Continua*. The struggle goes on. Be strong. Take it from someone that was on the outside looking in and now on the inside looking out.

You don't need a brick house to have a home. Now I have my husband, three kids and a fourth one on the way. I have my whole complete family living under one roof with no other parties having a say. Like the saying goes 'every dark cloud has a silver lining'. I found mine in Symphony Way.

Shamiela Mullins and family

To Whom it May Concern

MY HISTORY IN Life. This is how it begin.

I Michelle De Jongh, lives on Symphony Rd with my two children, Age 13 years and 8 years old, and my mother Age 66 yrs.

In 2004, we stayed at my cousin's place in Mitchell's Plain, along with her 3 children and husband. It was very terrible living like that, cause your children could never do what they pleases.

The first few weeks it was fine, but afterwards came the trouble, children trouble, arguments, etc. Although you pay your Rent and buy food everything goes wrong. Since then we moved to Bonteheuwel and the same thing happened.

The Heart of Struggle: A Pavement Exhibition, held on the barbed wire fence separating the community from the houses they once occupied, presented the professional work of independent photographer Antonio Angelucci side-by-side with the amateur work of the Symphony Way children. The child in the photo is one of contributors to this exhibition.

Myself, my children and my mother stayed in 12 places already. It is not worth it staying with people because theres always arguments and problems with the children, electricity and things like that.

Before we moved to the N2 Gateway Houses, we stayed in Roosendal, Delft. The lady that we stayed with was okay for the first two months, after that, we also had children problems. Her child would steal money and they would always say it was my children stealing the money.

I started attended Housing meetings without this woman knowing. Last year, every meeting there were, I attended. In December Counsillor Frank Martin kept meetings almost every night.

On the 19th December 2008 Frank Martin, told us to occupy the houses in N2 Gateway. Frank Martin also kicked a door open for a lady (elderly woman). We did put our furniture in the houses, some people paint their houses etc.

At night we sat outside at the fire, until the morning hours. On two nights we had to queue at the committies houses to pay for busses, or they will come fetch the money, so that we can go to Cape Town to court.

We were evicted twice and then we just moved our furniture back into the houses. The 19th February 2008, we were evicted by the Sheriff of the Court.

We moved our furniture and clothing and beds etc. to the field. The same afternoon I heard Frank Martin over the Radio saying he never told us to Occupy the houses, which he did.

That night we slept under the stars, whereas there were babies involved, pregnant woman, elderly people who were sick, etc. The next morning, we moved opposite the road, to stay on the pavement.

We are staying on this road for almost nine months.

We went through many things on the road, like example: We had trouble with car owners who pass by swearing and yelling at us when we tell them the road is closed. We had problems with law inforcement when they come on the road with their guns and the children they have fear. The children are really afraid of them when they see them because they come by force, swearing and threatening violence on the community.

Many more things happened on this road, like example: people had to go fetch wood in the bush, for food, fire. We organised games on the roads like soccer and netball. We had a modelling show with boys and girls and some mothers modelling and the parents watching.

We have sad and happy memories on this road. Symphony Way is a road which we will never forget.

Some people moved from here to the Tents and from there, they went to (Blikkiesdorp) TRA [Temporary Relocation Area]. We refuse to go to TRAs. We are here for houses not structures. The rest of us are still hoping for the best and we know we will succeed, cause we believe in God. We must just stick together so can be as a happy family. It is because of my desperation for a home that I'm on Symphony Way. Until today that I'm on the road, I still feel that God will provide us with houses.

We will wait until the end. We trust in God and ourselves as a community to help us through our struggle. I believe we will make a success.

Yours Sincerely
Miss M. De Jongh
Symphony Road
DELFT
7100
6 November 2008

Our Days of Struggle

EARLY IN DECEMBER we received letters from FRANK MARTIN to move into N2 Gateway Houses in Symphony Way Delft.

LATER we received information that we had been evicted out of our houses. It was very sad to move out because we were very excited in our houses. We had to go to court in Cape Town to fight for the houses. But we did not win the case so we had to move out. That same night we were evicted out of the houses we slept on the road. It was my first time I sleep on the street. During our Struggle we went through a lot. We survive threw the wind and storms. Thanks to God we made it till now. Me, Willem Hendricks, my wife Susan Hendricks, our sons William, Brandon, Marco, we really need a home. We believe in Ashraf because he stands by us threwly no matter what the situation my be. During our struggle [on the road] my 10 year old son was hit by car and broke his leg and had to go threw operation. He also had a know on the forehead but it wasnt serious – it was only bleading. It was very painful because we had to be there for him. And in the meantime we had to be on Symphony road as part of our struggle for houses. At that time, I wasn't here by the road. My eldest son called me at home. The guy that hit him, take him to the hospital. I was at the hospital and

they give me the phone number of the guy who him. So I wait the whole night till two o'clock to take him to Tygerberg Hospital. The next morning he had to go to operation. They put in a plate.

My youngest son also have asthma so I had to keep a close eye on him.

When we had stormy weather we cant sleep because it looks like the wind can blow our structure away. It was very scary during the night because we stay by the bush of evil, we dont know what can come out of the bushes. Early in November I had bad news about my mother who died suddenly. It was very heartbroken to lost my mother because she was always there when we need her.

During our Struggle a lot of people leave the road because they didn't believe in Ashraf. We believe Ashraf will go threw for us because we stand by him 100% and I believe God will work threw him to put us in our houses because we fighting for houses and not structures or 'blikkies' [shacks]. We are 12 yr on waiting list for a house I believe God will gift us our need. We all on Symphony road prayer every night because we are like one big family. Ashraf we love you because you are our hero. Because you put your family aside to be with us on the road.

No Land! No House! No Vote! Amandla!

Willem and Susan Hendricks

Marching to the High Court: No Land! No House! No Vote!

Die pad is toe

EK HET 'N baie goeie rede hoekom ek die huise beset het. Ek het nog nooit 'n huis gehad nie, my ouers het ook nog nooit een besit nie.

Ek is nou 23 jaar oud en is getroud en het twee kinders en 1 broer van 14 jaar oud. Ek kry swaar vandat ek kan ontdou, my ma het ook nog nooit 'n huis van haarself gehad nie. Ons het by baie mense gebly. Eers het ons in die Manenberg gebly daar waar die Tornado plaas gevind het. Ons het in Alfa Court gebly en toe gaan bly ons in die skool Silver Steam Primêr, na daai was ons na Phoenix Hoeër skool se velt en ons het daar gebly vir 6 jaar. Ons mense het die huise beset omdat ons graag huise will hê. Ons is moeg om te sien dat ander mense van ander lande kom en hulle word in ons huise gesit, hulle slaap lekker warm en ons wat hier gebore is moet by die bos bly op die pad. Hulle wat by die behuisings kantoor werk sê ons moet op die waglys wees en ons is daar op vir baie jare, nou wat ons gatvol is sê hulle daar bestaan nie meer 'n ding soos 'n wag lys nie. Nou hoekom het hulle ons in die eerste plek laat wag en wag? Ek is nou gatvol, want hulle doen nie hulle werk om vir ons huise gee nie. Ek kan dit nie bekostig om 'n hius te koop nie, want dit is vrek duur en ek werk nie!

Ek vertel julle hoe ek moet keer dat my kinders nie moet seer kry nie. My kinders kan nie speel in die pad nie as hulle speel dan kon die voertuie soos varke aan gery en ek bly vir hulle sê dat die pad is toe want ons bly hier op die pad. Elkeen wat hier aan kom wil vir ons seer maak want hulle wil deur kom want dit is 'n kort weg [ons maak hulle laat want ons maak die pad toe]. Ek bring ook kwaai vriendskap met die mense wat hier deur wil ry, hulle dreig elke dag vir my om my te skied want ek wil nie hê hulle moet deur kom nie. Ek moet elke dag en nag keer dat hulle nie moet deur kom nie, ek kry nooit rus nie die pad maak jou baie moegen siek.

Die ander ding is ek moet baie ver loop om vir ons water te kry, my rug kan dit nie meer hou niewant ek moet 'n baie swaar waterkan dra sodat ek genoeg water het om vir ons te was en kos te maak en ook wasgoed moet gewas word en ek moet opwas my liggaam is baie seer ek het nie meer krag daarvoor nie.

Maar ek staan hier totdat ek 'n huis kry vir ons almal. Ek sê NO LAND NO HOUSE NO VOTE, want wat is die rede om te VOTE maar jy kry nie 'n huis nie. Dit is vir die wêreld om te lees dat die Prisedent gee nie om vir ons mense nie, hulle wil vir ons T.R.A. Gee want moet ons daar maak dit is moes nie'n huis nie, dit is 'n silver blik wat nie gesond is vir ons kinders nie. Hulle word geryp en dood gemaak daarin want jy kan 'n mes vat en oop sny so din is daardie plate. Ek het my kinders baie lief en gaan nie sien dat hulle in daardie blik bly nie. Ek wil 'n huis hê waar ek weet my kinders slaap en hulle kan nie gepla word nie. Ek het baie kom leer op hierdie pad, ek het geleer dat jy moet nie staat maak op

die mense wat sê hulle gaan vir jou help om 'n huis te kry, maar hulle doen nie soos hulle sê nie.

Elke dag kom hier mense van orals om te sien hoe ons bly en vra baie vrae. Ons sê vir hulle dat dit is nie lekker om hier op die pad en in blikkies te woon niewant ons kinders raak elke dag stouter want hulle begin te dink dat dit is hoe ons moet bly, en ek dink dat dit is nie goed om ons kinders so groot te laat word nie. Ek sal nooit hiedie dag vergeet nie. Dit was die 24/3/2008 toe ek my wasgoed gewas het.

Ek het mos nie 'n huis met 'n agtergrond nic, toe besluit ek gaan vir my wasgoed lyne maak in die pad en ons klere in die pad op hang, en toe ek klaar op gehang het kom daar 'n polisie kar en hy klim toe uit en maak my lynne los en ek sê vir hom hy weet mos die pad is toe want ons mense het nie herberg nie. En die ander rede hoekom die pad toe is is omdat die staat saamgestem het met die community om die pad regtig toe te maak. Toe sit hulle die barriers, en die pad is dus so te se toe. Ek vat die lyn uit sy hand en hy gryp vir my voor die bors en vra of ek weet wie hy is, hy gaan vir my toesliut as ek nie die pad gaan oop maak nie. Ek sê vir hom maar die pad is mos toe hy kan nie my wasgoed op die grond gooi nie, want dit is baie harde werk om dit weer te was, toe wys hy vir my dat hy is 'n polisie man ek kan vir hom niks maak nie en gooi al my wasgoed op die grond en ry oor dit. Ek het gedog ek gaan mal raak want ek moes maar net dit optel en in my badtjie sit en weer water moet gaan haal. Dit was 'n baie hardseer dag om te dink jy het niks regtes in die staad se oë nie jy is maar net 'n stuk kak en gedierte in hulle oë.

Op die 2/7/2008 het my kinders op die taaiers in die pad gespeel en die taaiers vol sand gegooi toe kom daar 'n rooi Opel aan en daar was twee mans in, en klim uit en stoot my kinders laat hulle twee met hulle gesigte op die grond neer val. Toe ek sien hulle maak my kinders seer want hulle kan nie vir hulle self beskerm nie, het ek vir hulle gesê dat ek gaan vir hulle toe laat sluit want hulle kan nie kinders wil seer maak nie. Toe kom die een nader aan my en steek my met 'n skroewerdryer en wil my kinders ook steek, maar ek tel toe 'n klip op en gooi vir hom en sy motor en skree vir help, maar niemand kon vir my hoor nie, toe kom daar 'n polisie motor aan en hulle sien dat ek makeer help en toe klim die twee mans in die motor en hardloop weg. Toe die polisie by my kom toe sien hulle dat ek by die hospitaal moet kom maar ek wou nie saam gaan nie. Ek het besluit ek gaan by my hok bly en kyk na my kinders, Hulle sê vir my hulle kan niks doen as ek nie wil saam met hulle wil gaan nie. Ek sê vir hulle ek gaan weer seer kry so lank soos ons hier bly want dit is mos nie 'n huis waar ek weet ek kan my deur toe sluit en lekker rus nie.

Dit was op 'n Sondag oggend, toe ek besig gewees het met my kos en my man was buitekant besig om sy voertuig te was. Kom daar 'n kar aan met een man en twee vrou-mense en die man klim toe uit met 'n glas vol bier. Hy wil toe oop maak en ek gaan na hom en sê " sir, the road is closed" (meneer, die pad is gesluit), hy sê toe vir my " voetsek! " en lig daai swaar sand tyre en ons keer hom en hy vra vir my "waar is my tande? Ek moet sy penis kom lek" . Toe hoor my man dit en hardloop na hom met die besemstok. En my neighbour kom met die piksteel en wil vir hom slaan want hy kan nie so praat met ander vrouens nie. Hy sê toe " sorry, sorry!" en klim in sy motor en ry.

Om op hierdie pad te bly is dit baie baie swaar maar wat help dit om te kla want hulle by die behuisings doen nie hul werk nie.

Kashifa Jacobs
Sedick Jacobs
Zakeer Jacobs
Sedeeqa Jacobs
Symphony Way
Delft
7100
3 November 2008

*The Symphony
Way 'beach'*

The gang

Amandla Ngawethu! The power is ours! Join us...

With our dogs

The road is closed

I HAD A good reason why I invaded the house. I never had a home of my own, not even my parents had a house.

I am now 23 years old and married with two children and one brother that is 14 years old. For as long as I can remember I have been suffering, my mother never had a house of herself. We stayed by a lot of people. First we stayed in Manenberg, thats where the Tornado happened. We stayed in Alfa Court and so we went to stay in Silver Steam Primary School, and after that we went to go stay in Phoenix High School on the field where we stayed for six years. We invaded the houses because we truly needed homes. We are tired to see that people from other lands are put in the houses that belongs to us, they sleeping lekker [nicely] in the warmth while we that are born here have to sleep in the bush and on the streets. The ones that are working by the housing department said we have to be on waiting lists and we are it for years, and now we are gatvol [fed up], now they say the waiting list doesn't exist. How come did they let us wait and wait? I am now gatvol, because they don't do their work to give us homes. I can't afford to buy a house, because it is vrek [too expensive] and I'm not working!

I tell them how I have to prevent my children from getting hurt. When my children play on the road and then the cars ride like pigs and I keep on telling them [the drivers] that the road is closed because we stay here. Everybody that rides through here want to hurt us because its a short road to get where they want to be [and we are making them late by blocking the road]. I am getting kwaai [dangerous] enemies because I dont want them to ride through. They threatened to shoot me because I block the road. Everyday and night I have to stop them to ride through – this road makes you sick and tired.

The other thing is I must walk far to go and fetch water, my back can't take it anymore because I have to carry very heavy water cans so that we can have enough water to wash [ourselves], and to cook, and to wash the washing. And my body is very sore through carrying heavy water cans and my body has no more strength.

But I stand until we all get houses. And I say NO LAND NO HOUSE NO VOTE, because what is the reason to VOTE, if we don't get houses. That is for the world to read, that the President does not care for the people who is struggling, but now they want to give us T.R.A.s [Temporary Relocation Areas]. What must we do there because it is not homes, it is just a silver tin thats not healthy for our kids. Some people get rapes and get killed in this tins because you can use a nife to cut through the plate (of the tins). I love my children so much, I won't let them live in those tin houses. I need a house where I know my children won't be disturbed while they are sleeping. I learned a lot on the road and I have also

137

learned not to trust people that say they will help you to get a house and don't keep their promises and do nothing about it.

Everyday there is people that come from everywhere and ask many questions, then we tell them its not lekker to stay on the road and in the blikkies [tin cans]. While we staying here in this informal settlement, our children learn a lot of bad tings and get naughty day by day because they think its the normal way of living. I don't think it is right for our children to stay in this way. I will never forget 24/3/2008, what happened on that day. When I was busy washing my washing, I decided to hang my clothes over the road because we haven't got a place to hang our washing. While I was busy, there was a police car coming around and they decided to take off my temporary washing lines while I was busy. I told them the road was closed because we doesn't have any place to stay. The other reason why the road is closed is because the state agreed with the community who stay on the pavement, that the road is closed. They put also barriers, thats why the road is closed. I took the line out of his hand and he grabbed me in front of my chest and asked me, do I know who he is, and he will lock me up if I don't open the road. I told him the road is closed and he is not going to throw my washing on the ground because its very hard work to wash it again. Then, he show me that he is a policeman and that I can't do him nothing and threw all my washing on the ground and ride over it. I thought that I gonna get mad but I just had to pick up my badtjie [washing basin] and I had to go and fetch more water. I was so heart-sore to think that you have no rights in the eyes of the state and you are a stuk kak [piece of shit] and an animal in their eyes.

On the 2/7/2008 [2nd of July]. My children played on the tyres and put some sand in the tyres and there came a red Opel with two men inside. Then, they climbed out, they push my children, that they fall with their faces down to the ground. When I saw they hurt my children I told them I will let them be locked up because my children can't defend themselves because they are hurting them. Then one of these men stab me with the screwdriver and also want to stab my children. And then I pick up a stone and throw it to him and his car and was crying for help but no one did hear me. Seeing that I needed help, a police car came, the two men climbed in their car and drove away. When the police came, they saw that I needed to go to the hospital but I refused to go with them. I decided to stay by my shack and look after my children. They said they can't do nothing if I don't want to go with them. I told them that I will get hurt again as long as I stay here because this is not a house where I can just lock my door and rest lekker.

On the Sundy morning while I was busy with my food for the day and my husband was busy washing his vehicle outside, then there was a vehicle arriving with one man and two women and the man climb out of the car with a glass of beer. He want to open the barriers but I go to him and tell him, 'Sir, the road is

closed'. Then he told me 'voetsek' [fuck off] and picked up the tyre with sand in it and we tried to stop him and he was asking *where is my teath, I must come and suck his penis*. My husband heard and ran to him with a broomstick. And my neighbours come there with pickax and they wanted to hit him because he can't speak to other women like that. Then he said *sorry, sorry*, and climbed in his car and drive away.

To stay on this road is very hard, but what does it help to complain because the housing department don't do their work.

Kashifa Jacobs
Sedick Jacobs
Zakeer Jacobs
Sedeeqa Jacobs
Symphony Way
Delft
7100
3 November 2008

Our tap: Symphony Way kids collect water for our families

Postscript

Symphony Way is not dead.
We are still Symphony Way.
We will always be Symphony Way

Press release issued by the Symphony Way Anti-Eviction Campaign

30 October 2009

WE, THE PAVEMENT dwellers of Symphony Way, have just completed our forced removed from the road into the relocation camp of Blikkiesdorp.[1] However, during the past week, a lot of misinformation has been thrown around about our community by the City and in the media.

Firstly, we would like to make absolutely clear that there was not a single family from Symphony Way who actually wanted to move to Blikkiesdorp. It was reported in the Argus a few days ago that people were excited about their new places and the move was festive. This is of course not true. There is a reason that over 100 families actively refused to move to Blikkies for over 20 months. It was also reported that there were divisions in the community about the move. This is also untrue. We were merely having an extended conversation of our options: (a) pay exhorbitant fees at backyards, (b) go to crime infested Blikkies, (c) occupy unused land, occupy empty bond houses, etc. The only reason we have moved to Blikkiesdorp is because our children are traumatised by the first eviction in February 2008[2] in which police opened fire and shot over 20 of us including women and children.[3] We do not want our families to again face the violence of this evil police force.

Now that we have moved to Blikkiesdorp, we are not happy about the conditions. Many of our toilets and taps are not working. Many of our roofs are faulty and substandard.

In Symphony Way, there was almost no crime and we left our doors unlocked.
In Blikkies the crime is out of control and we barricade ourselves in our homes at night.

In Symphony Way, it was warmer because we had better insulation from the cold.
In Blikkies, the shacks have no significant insulation.

In Symphony Way, it was less windy.
In Blikkies, the wind blows the sand in our faces and hair

In Symphony Way, larger families built larger structures
In Blikkies, all the structures are the same no matter the family size

Therefore, we wish to extend a cordial invitation to those responsible for the reimergence of Apartheid era Temporary Relocation Areas in the new South Africa. We would like to invite Plato, Zille, Sexwale and any government official to spend a week living in the Symphony Section of Blikkiesdorp (not just a day because that is just a PR campaign[4]). Perhaps, this way, you will finally understand why we hate Blikkiesdorp so much. And dont worry, we will protect you from the drug dealers and rapists!

Our Way Forward: We wish to make known that we are still the Symphony Way Pavement Dwellers. We may not be living on the road, but our fight for houses *has only just begun*. We warn government that we have not forgotten that they have promised us houses and we, the Symphony Way Anti-Eviction Campaign, will make sure we get what is rightfully ours. We will be holding a mass meeting of Symphony Block this Sunday the 1st of November to decide as a community on the way forward for our struggle. You may call us to find out what we have decided.

Notes

1. 'Photos: "Blikkiesdorp", the Symphony Way TRA', Western Cape Anti-Eviction Campaign, http://antieviction.org.za/2009/01/18/photos-blikkiesdorp-the-symphony-way-tra/, accessed 28 April 2010.
2. Kerry Chance (2008) 'Housing and Evictions at the N2 Gateway Project in Delft: A Report for Abahlali baseMjondolo', Western Cape Anti-Eviction Campaign, 8 May, http://antieviction.org.za/2008/05/21/housing-and-evictions-at-the-n2-gateway-project-in-delft/, accessed 28 April 2010.
3. Verashni Pillay (2008) 'Delft residents stranded', Western Cape Anti-Eviction Campaign, 19 February, http://antieviction.org.za/2008/02/19/delft-residents-stranded/, accessed 28 April 2010.
4. Verashni Pillay (2008).